Make Your Web Site Work for You

Also by CommerceNet Press:

Opening Digital Markets: Battle Plans and Business Strategies for Internet Commerce by Walid Mougayar
The Search for Digital Excellence by James P. Ware et al.
StrikingItRich.com by Jaclyn Easton
The Future of Work by Charles Grantham
How to Invest in E-Commerce Stocks by Bill Burnham and Piper Jaffray
Understanding Digital Signatures: Establishing Trust Over the Internet and Other Networks by Gail Grant
Building Database-Driven Web Catalogs by Sherif Danish and Patrick Gannon
Buying a Car on the Internet by Jeremy Lieb
Buying a Home on the Internet by Robert Irwin
Buying Travel Services on the Internet by Durant Imboden
Understanding SET: Visa International's Official Guide to Secure Electronic Transactions by Gail Grant

CommerceNet is a nonprofit industry consortium for companies promoting and building electronic commerce solutions on the Internet. Launched in April 1994 in Silicon Valley, CA, its membership has grown to more than 500 companies and organizations worldwide. They include the leading banks, telecommunications companies, VANs, ISPs, online services, software and service companies, as well as end-users, who together are transforming the Internet into a global electronic marketplace. For membership information, please contact CommerceNet at Tel: 408-446-1260; Fax: 408-446-1268; URL: htp://www.commerce.net. For information regarding CommerceNet Press contact Loël McPhee at loel@commerce.net.

Make Your Web Site Work for You

HOW TO CONVERT YOUR ONLINE CONTENT INTO PROFITS

JEFF CANNON

CommerceNet Press

McGraw-Hill

New York   San Francisco   Washington, D.C.   Auckland   Bogotá
Caracas   Lisbon   London   Madrid   Mexico City   Milan
Montreal   New Dehli   San Juan   Singapore
Sydney   Tokyo   Toronto

Library of Congress Catalog Card Number: 99-75155

McGraw-Hill

A Division of The McGraw-Hill Companies

2 3 4 5 6 7 8 9 0   AGM/AGM   0 9 8 7 6 5 4 3 2 1 0

ISBN 0-07-135241-4

This book was set in Palatino by BookMasters, Inc.

Printed and bound by Quebecor Martinsburg.

McGraw-Hill books are available at special quality discounts to use as premiums and sales promotions, or for use in corporate training programs. For more information, please write to the Director of Special Sales, McGraw-Hill, Professional Publishing, Two Penn Plaza, New York, NY 10121-2298. Or contact your local bookstore.

This book is printed on recycled, acid-free paper containing a minimum of 50% recycled de-inked fiber.

*This book is dedicated to Walt and Weta,
whose endless support continues to make
anything and everything possible, and to my
brothers Jon and Marc and my wife Laura,
who never cease to inspire.*

Contents

Foreword

If your business isn't online already, run—don't walk—to your nearest ISP. And if your business isn't engaging in, or at least seriously exploring electronic commerce, now is the time.

The learning curve is steep, the pitfalls are many, and the investment doesn't come cheap, yet stragglers and laggards will be left on the I-way like so much cyber-roadkill.

Companies that are quick to try, to learn, to adapt—and to make the inevitable mistakes—will win.

Some of the biggest successes on the Internet today began their journey many years ago, long before it was thought possible to make a single dollar off the Internet. The brokerage firm Charles Schwab, for example, began offering online stock trading to its clients back in 1984, fully a decade before the Web's commercial birth. With this much learning under its belt, Schwab was able to grow from 336,000 online accounts in 1995 to 1.6 million in May of 1998.

And it's not just large companies that are reaping the benefits. Small businesses can now get their feet wet with ecommerce for as little as $25 a month by taking advantage of storefront hosting services.

There are three major power shifts in our midst that will make the Internet an even bigger opportunity (or threat) for online businesses over the next several years. These are:

Power Shift Number One: From Large to Small Businesses

Over the next couple of years, there will be a major movement online among small businesses. The Internet will eventually serve as the great equalizer, giving small firms the opportunity to reach a truly global audience at a substantially reduced cost.

As management guru Peter Drucker has said, "The Fortune 500 is over." Of course, he wasn't suggesting the Fortune 500 will go away, merely that the advantage of being huge will no longer be as important as it once was. At the beginning of this century, giant corporations were created to exploit vast economies of scale in manufacturing and distribution. But now that our economy is focused more on services and information, particularly digital information, economies of scale are less critical.

Power Shift Number Two: From Sellers to Buyers

The Web—in a way no other medium can—allows for the free flow of information on price, product, delivery, distribution, and payment terms, resulting in what Bill Gates calls "friction-free capitalism." This will inevitably put more power in the hands of the buyers of our economy—both business buyers and end-user consumer buyers.

Increasing numbers of businesses are participating in, or creating, value-added trading centers. Business-to-business intermediaries are emerging and setting up vast electronic commerce hubs to bring thousands of buyers and sellers together for the purpose of exchanging information for price quotes, placing bids, providing customer service, and conducting actual transactions over the Net.

Power Shift Number Three: From Direct Sellers to Intermediaries

Aggregation, particularly in the context of the Internet, is not a new concept, but aggregation predicated on a particular customer's needs and wants is new and different.

Imagine walking into a supermarket where everything is arranged, not by product category, but by company manufacturer. All of the Procter & Gamble products, from toothpaste to cold remedies, are in one display aisle, and all the Colgate-Palmolive brands are in another. Comparing toothpaste would mean running back and forth between aisles.

Entirely new businesses will emerge dedicated to aggregating content for a particular type of customer. These businesses may not have any relation to, or even an understanding of, the industry or market segment they aggregate, but they will know their customer and what he or she is seeking.

The Internet is the most customer-centric medium we have ever seen, but it seems many online businesses have not grasped this concept.

You can create a Web site for your business; invest thousands of dollars in an elaborate, state-of-the-art ecommerce system; purchase banner ads on all the "right" portals and niche-targeted sites; but if you fail to listen to your customer and provide them with the information they are looking for, you are doomed to failure.

The Internet is like any other medium. Like television, radio, or print, it is a component to be incorporated in a marketing campaign, not as a stand-alone. This does not mean you should not be on the Web. It means you also need to rely on traditional media. Consider the Internet as an add-on to your traditional media mix. Treat the Internet as a part of your business, not an electronic hole in the ground in which to throw precious marketing dollars.

With this book, Mr. Cannon has created an outline for doing this— for building an online presence that makes business sense. Keep in mind some of the trends I have outlined. Apply them to your online plans. Most important, do it quickly, because this kind of opportunity only comes along once in a lifetime.

Geoffrey Ramsey
Statsmaster—eMarketer

Preface
A Letter from Leo Burnett

The following memo was written in 1948 by one of the greatest names in advertising—Leo Burnett. I have included it because it, better than any letter or article written today, expresses the doubt, pain, and questions everyone is facing with the Internet. It also shows the opportunities that wait for those with the foresight to explore the possibilities and think constructively outside the box.

TELEVISION

(From a memorandum by Leo Burnett to members of the executive staff)

I realize that the way I feel about television is no secret to you, but if possible I want to give you in this memo some of the depth of my conviction about it.

Many of you may recall how I felt about *Life* magazine in its early days, but really that enthusiasm was a passing fancy compared to my feeling about television.

In my opinion television is the greatest medium of mass communication since the invention of the printing press.

—the most powerful means of selling, second only to personal demonstrations

—and I am willing to put my neck out to the extent of predicting that within 10 years it will be the world's number one advertising medium in terms of goods sold.

*   *   *   *   *   *

Personal Experience

No matter how many television shows you have seen in bars or anywhere else, you don't really get under the weight of this thing until you get a television set in your own home.

The set is turned on whenever there is a program to look at and listen to.

You come home and find your living room full of strangers who have dropped in to have a look.

The kids who used to be gallivanting around the neighborhood are right there (sitting on the floor) with their eyes glued to the set.

All programs and all commercials seem to be interesting to everybody.

My 82-year-old mother-in-law is fascinated with "Junior Jamboree" in the afternoon and my teen-age daughter is just as interested in the Great Books program discussing Plato, et al., on Thursday nights.

Maybe it isn't a good thing for our civilization that refined and respectable women should be fascinated by flying mares, half gainers and kangaroo kicks in the wrestling program on Monday nights, but anyway they are.

I could go on and on with such experiences but I mention them here only because I feel they express the vitality of this great new medium.

Novelty, you say.

Yes, it is novel and almost incomprehensible that the waves from something that is happening 50 miles away should form themselves into the perfect pattern of sight and sound right in your own living room.

But here's the way I feel about novelty.

Maybe a year from now television will have become more of a habit and less of a phenomenon in my home. Maybe we won't watch it quite so much. But in the meantime this same experience will be taking place in thousands of other homes where new sets have been installed.

While the circulation is building, in my opinion the novelty (if you want to call it that) will last for at least 5 years.

Two and Two Don't Make Four

Another thing is the depth of impression delivered by television.

If you want to count an impression received through the eye as two and an impression received through the ear as two, they don't add up to four—but to six or eight or something.

One impression helps the other and you actually remember what was shown and said.

Even Poor Television Is Good

Some of the stuff you see on the television today is pretty amateurish, I grant you—*but you sit there and look at it just the same.*

When shown on television, commercials that would irritate and bore you over the radio become actually interesting.

Part of our job as an agency is to improve the technique of television commercials and, take it from me, we are going to, but in the meantime even a poor or mediocre television job has a vitality and a depth of impression that you don't get out of the best printed ad or the best radio commercial.

"Simple Drama" Come into Its Own

In planning printed advertising, particularly magazine pages in order, we have always said to ourselves that every product has simple drama and that our job is to capture it and interpret it rather than to employ a lot of phony devices to get what we call "readership."

Here in television that opportunity is greatly multiplied.

The best television commercials, as I have observed them, are those that actually show and demonstrate the product—the poorest are those which employ trick devices, presumably to get attention or to entertain.

Mentally I have just gone over all the accounts in our shop. I cannot think of a single one of them which does not lend itself to this natural convincing treatment.

Learning Through Doing

As you know, we expect to learn television through *doing.*

We don't want a client who has just put a television set in his home to call up some day and ask, "What are you fellows doing about television?" and be obliged to tell him vaguely that we are "studying" it or "keeping abreast of it."

You are not abreast of television today unless you are on the air with it, and it is our desire that each and every one of our clients should be on television in some form within the next 6 months.

＊　＊　＊　＊　＊　＊

My opinion is that right now—today—television can be made to pay its way as an advertising medium—not to mention the experience it gives you and the priority it establishes for you on leadership stations at desirable time periods.

What it lacks in circulation it makes up in depth of impression and vitality.

As for the future—my own opinion is that through television entirely new sales levels, which might seem fantastic today, will be attained by those who use it and use it right.

Introduction

Making Money by Working a Plan

Are people making money on the Internet or is it just a global pipe dream? It's the question everyone has been asking since the world got wired. It's also a question that can be answered with certainty.

The truth is people are making money on the Internet. People are starting online publications that reach millions of readers. People are creating new opportunities for stagnant products. In short, people are turning ideas into profits, and profits into businesses on the World Wide Web. If you doubt any of this, read on. You will read the success stories in this book.

Regardless of whether you want to turn an idea into a profitable business, leverage the Internet to grow an existing business, or create a successful Web presence, this book will help you do two things. First, avoid the mistakes others have made, and second, make the idea profitable.

For you, and hundreds like you, the million dollar question is not, "Should I get on the Net?" but rather, "What is the secret to success online?" The answer is simple: Those who are making money online are doing it the same way businesses have been making money for years—by taking proven rules of business and adapting them to the changing business world.

The lessons and case studies in this book will surprise you, not because of leading edge technology, but by how low tech the solutions are. People created some of the most successful online businesses with little or no computer experience. With each case study you will find nobody reinvented the wheel; instead, they rebuilt the cart.

You will also see that success on the Internet is not just a matter of building a Web site—for some, a Web site isn't even a part of their business. Online success is a matter of creating a business plan and sticking to it, of seeing the pitfalls and avoiding them, of using the elements of the Internet that make sense and avoiding those that will only waste time and money.

No, this book is not a ticket to overnight success. It is a guide to taking your idea online and creating a successful business. It will show you how to use the tools the Internet provides, and it will show you how to avoid some of the pitfalls other people have already found.

The Internet is a place to turn ideas into success. The question to ask yourself is not whether you can build a successful online business. The question is, are you willing to put in the time and energy that it requires?

Consumers to Customers, Customers to Profits

The first question everyone asks, is why go on the Internet at all? The answer is simple—because starting a business on the Internet is quicker, easier, and less expensive than doing it offline. Even more important, the Internet provides a flexible arena in which to test and sell your product, enabling you the ability to refine your plans to meet your customer's needs as they change—and they will.

Success on the Internet is not about the newest fads, the coolest trick, the hottest technology, or the fastest site. It is about building a name to which people recognize and respond. It is about responding to customers' needs and providing them with the information they are seeking and selling them on the value of a product. Success on the Internet is not about reinventing the wheel, but about doing the same thing successful companies have been doing for years—creating relationships that turn consumers into customers, and customers into loyal brand buyers.

Companies like Disney, Nike, and Barnes & Noble have spent millions to build brick and mortar stores filled with logos and brand icons to build these kinds of relationships. They have created Disney Stores and Niketowns across the country where the sole objective is to get consumers excited enough to make a purchase.

The Internet is able to do the same thing. It can create branded environments able to excite consumers enough to buy. What this means is a marketing tool that was once only available to the largest of corporations is now available to everyone. If you doubt the power of this, just visit Amazon.com—a company that did not exist several years ago. It is now competing against the largest book dealers in the world. To approach the Web expecting anything less is to miss the full potential of the World Wide Web as a business tool.

Yes, the Internet is a growing communications medium. Yes, it does have a long way to go before we realize its full potential, but it is already a very powerful medium that brings with it a number of very real benefits. Now is not the time to wait. Regardless of the form the Internet takes in the future, now is the time to start using it and leveraging it as a very crucial part of every marketing mix.

Using This Book

Make Your Web Site Work for You is written for three types of people:

- The person with an idea who wants to build a new business using the World Wide Web
- The businessperson with an offline product or service who wants to take it online
- The marketing executive who wants to promote their brand through the Internet

Make Your Web Site Work for You uses the sales cycle as its guideline to building an online business. The reason for this is simple: regardless of whether you are selling a product or starting a publication, everything you do to generate revenue will fall into the sales cycle at some time. Whether you are selling advertising or selling a product, your goal is to bring advertisers and consumers together in an ad-friendly environment. If you don't understand where the opportunities are, you will miss them—and the opportunities begin long before a credit card is ever pulled out

As you read, you will find you recognize many of the concepts in this book. The reason is simple: you have seen them in the past. I am not presenting any new ideas that are not founded on proven marketing concepts. Again, the reason is simple: they work. However, you will notice they have been changed and adapted to meet the nature of the Internet. These adaptations are based on the trials and errors of existing online businesses. For this reason, if you see something that looks familiar to you and feel you can skip the section, I urge you to at least skim the content. Otherwise, you may fall into the trap many have learned—lessons from the traditional business world do not necessarily apply without some changes to them.

This book is divided into seven key areas:

1. **The Basics**—This covers the basic rules for online marketing. It includes an overview of the sales cycle and the reasons why content marketing works. Read them. For the business owner, this will provide the basis for starting an online business, and for the marketing executive, this will provide the rationale of why, or why not, a specific product should be taken online.

2. **The First Step to Going Online: Developing a Brand**—Primarily for the business owner, this section takes a step-by-step approach to taking an idea and turning it into a branded product. Regardless of how well you know your product, this may be one of the most important steps to understanding the how and why of creating a successful product on-, or offline

3. **Building Online Content to Drive Your Business**—This section teaches you how to create content that attracts consumers to your site and encourages them to respond regardless of what you are trying to sell or promote.

4. **Driving Traffic and Keeping It in Your Online Store**—These are the ways and means to driving traffic to your site. Banner ads? Think again.

5. **Preparing Your Site to Profit**—Whether you are selling advertising, creating ecommerce for products, or developing subscriptions, this is what you will need to do.

6. **Research and Customer Service**—Creating a real relationship with your customers means long-term success. It also means taking your site out of the box and putting it into the consumer's hands. It is the most important part of an online marketing and sales program that works.

7. **Case Studies and Resources**—Although references to Web sites are included throughout the book, these are the full stories behind their success. In addition, there are links for online resources that will provide you with the most updated news and information for building and maintaining a successful online business.

Each of these sections follows a basic outline of theory and implementation. Each chapter will discuss the concepts it is based on and then moves through a step-by-step program to implement those concepts in the real world. Each includes case studies and real-world examples to allow you to see what real online companies have done.

As you go through this book, you will find that many of the concepts overlap. Tools that can be used to promote a site can also be used to integrate research into the content. Tools that can be used to create content can also be used to develop a community. As essential to knowing which tools to use is knowing how to leverage one tool to achieve several objectives. Not only does this create a more integrated campaign, it creates fewer interruptions for your visitors.

There are many references in this book to various technologies such as bulletin boards, chat engines, email lists, and database software. Most are available on the Internet. To find them, your best bet will be to go to some of the Web sites that offer free software or programming codes that are listed in the appendixes. However, if you are unsure how to implement them, it is best to work with a consultant or programmer who can do so. Keep in mind these technologies will change. The Internet itself will change. In a year, I will not be surprised if you find a particular technology somewhat outdated or surpassed with another application. If so, use the one best suited to your needs, but apply the concepts that are presented. They work, and they will not change over time.

Last of all, I offer a reality check. I personally believe the Internet is one of the greatest creations this world has seen since the wheel. It has the capability of bringing people together from around the world in an exchange of thoughts and ideas never dreamed of before. However, like human nature, it has a dark side, so be careful with whom you deal and with how you develop your online business. If you would refrain from dealing with a business offline, refrain from doing so online. Don't be afraid to ask for references, and always fully explore any Web site you are thinking of partnering. A little common sense will go a long way.

In all, be persistent and stay true to your dreams. You will trip along the way. You will hit some snags, but they are not things others haven't experienced to an even greater degree than you have. Regardless of how much you plan, everything will not work out according to it. You will have to be flexible, but maintain your vision and be persistent and you will succeed.

As you will see, persistence of vision pays off, often in ways you never imagined.

Jeff Cannon

Acknowledgments

Since joining the Internet in the early '90s, I have had the pleasure of working with some truly brilliant people. What makes each of them unique is not the ability to program a Web site or even their email, but their ability to recognize their strengths and having the insight to compensate for the rest by nurturing the best and the brightest. There are many more people who deserve thanks for helping me develop this book and my business than are listed here, but this is at least a start.

Foremost, I would like to thank Jaclyn Easton, one of the few people I would consider a mentor, and quite possibly one of the brightest people I know. Suffice it to say her wisdom, guidance, and humor extends far beyond the walls of the Internet.

I would like to also thank Loel McPhee. Not only has she provided the insight in writing this book, she has guided me around the pitfalls and traps that lay between the ideas and the pages.

I remain impressed by the people I met during my tenure with the *Los Angeles Times.* Of these, two stand out in particular, Carol Perruso and Leah Gentry. I continually admire both, not only for their skill and business savvy, but for their ability to bring a human element into an otherwise frenetic world. Just some of the others from that team who provided me with more hats than anyone could hope to wear are Harry Chandler, Stan Holt, Travis Smith, and Donna Stokley.

I would also like to extend a debt of gratitude to a former *Los Angeles Times* executive, Bob Brisco. His skill and business sense are matched only by his understanding of what is truly important. Thank you.

One of the first people I met upon arriving in Silicon Alley was Alice O'Rourke, president of the New York News Media Association. I remain in constant awe of her ability to calmly navigate a rather large ship in what can be a sometimes treacherous ocean. Thank you for helping to build Silicon Alley.

To Gail and Howard Sonnenschein and the entire Bikini.com staff, I would like to thank you for your constant support in my writing this book and for providing me with a tropical atoll 365 days a year.

To Steve Kolker and Paul Posnick who have two of the best minds the advertising industry has seen in years and a rare combination of foresight, experience, and youthful exuberance that enables them to go far outside the box—thank you.

To Rennie Sloan, Ginger Thoerner, and the rest of the *U.S. News & World Report* staff to whom I owe a great debt of thanks for being instrumental in growing my business and my knowledge.

To Leo Burnett for establishing many of the rules that still apply today and to Betty Redmond and Sheri Carpenter for helping me pass his wisdom to a new generation.

To Christine Bourron, Stratis Morfogen, Andrew Peck, and Ken Seiff, I owe great thanks for working with me to develop the case studies incorporated into this book.

I would also like to thank Geoffrey Ramsey and eMarketer for providing me with the statistics and background information that supported much of my work.

Last, but most important, I would like to thank my father and his friends from the advertising world of the '60s who taught me what this wacky industry is really all about.

Make Your Web Site
Work for You

CHAPTER ONE

The Basics

THE SALES CYCLE

More than 2,400 years ago, Sun Tzu, one of the world's first and most renowned writers on the subject of war wrote, "a victorious army wins its victories before seeking battle." The same is true in the business world. Almost every product is sold before the customer ever enters a store, but to do this you must understand the sales cycle.

The sales cycle is one of the most basic components of running a business on- or offline. The fact is, everything we do from product development to packaging, advertising, selling, and finally customer service is done to affect the consumer's purchase decision. Yet many of us wait until the customer walks into a store before they start selling. In doing so most businesses miss some of the best opportunities to actually sell.

By understanding the sales cycle, not only will you understand where the opportunities to sell exist, you will understand how to capture a consumer and turn them into a customer before your competition has the chance to and before they ever enter your on- or offline store.

Throughout the sales cycle every company has two objectives. First, they must ensure the consumer maintains the decision to purchase a given product. Second, they must ensure the final purchase decision is to buy a specific product.

As you go through each phase of the sales cycle, don't think in terms of selling a product. Think how long it takes you to make a decision to

1

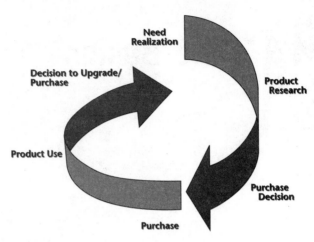

The Sales Cycle

buy a product. Then look for the opportunity to affect the decision of someone buying your product. This rarely includes offering a product earlier in the cycle. More often it means creating a relationship that the consumer will return to when it comes time to purchase.

Need Realization

The sales cycle starts when the consumer first recognizes their need for a product or service. This may be as simple as being thirsty and realizing the need for a drink. It may be as difficult as realizing the current computer system is not able to keep up with customer orders. Regardless of the purchase, the fight for a sale has begun.

Today, most consumers are aware of the most popular brands offered. If someone is looking for a drink, they are aware of what is available. If someone is looking for a computer, they are probably aware of the leading products and some of the key benefits that each provides. Thanks to the category leaders who have spent heavily in advertising and whose names are easily recognized, the consumer's introduction to a specific category has been made.

In general, the greater a brand's presence in the general market, the more likelihood of consumer recognition, and the greater chance of consideration during the next phase of the sales process. However, this does not mean the fight for a sale has been won. If used carefully, this advantage can be turned against them. Just think how many people from IBM or Apple are willing to spend time on the phone with a prospective sale to see what their concerns are and respond to their needs. In the mind of most consumers, big equals unapproachable, and this creates an opportunity.

Product Research

Once someone recognizes their need, they enter into some form of research. At this point the consumer assesses their specific needs and begins to rate each product based on its ability to fulfill their needs. A product's ability to satisfy a need is the product's benefits.

Depending on the urgency of the purchase, the consumer will go through a process of collecting and processing as much information as they can to make an intelligent decision. For lesser purchases, this may be as simple as availability and consideration of known brands (e.g., What soda is available on the grocer's shelf? How adventurous do I feel?). For more involved purchases, this may take the form of calling business associates for product recommendations, sending out RFPs, taking products for a test drive, researching on- and offline publications, or a combination of these. Every product is considered based on its ability to serve a consumer's needs. Considerations begin in broad terms and become more refined as the process continues.

At this point in the sales process, stronger brands that have advertised heavily will have a significant lead, and since a product's brand affects how people feel about a product's reputation, reliability, and prestige, it will continue to affect the consumer's purchase.

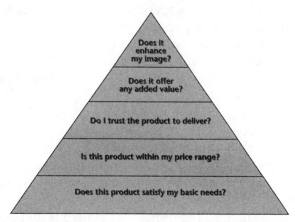

Considerations to a Purchase Decision

However, the research phase is also the point where a smaller brand can begin to influence a consumer's purchase decision. As we have said, it can do this by starting a relationship with the consumer. How does it do this? It provides them with the information they are seeking. It helps them make an intelligent purchase decision, and in so doing, simultaneously promotes their own product benefits.

As you will see, consumers respond to companies that want to partner with them when making their purchase decision. It's called developing a relationship with the consumer.

Purchase Decision

The final purchase decision is a result of the consumer analyzing his or her research. This not only includes quantitative research such as price and perceived value, it also includes qualitative factors such as reputation and prestige. Factors come into play from a variety of sources, each having various levels of importance attached to them.

A person's personal opinions about what is important weigh heavily, followed by the opinions of family, peer and social groups, and then by culture and sub-cultural trends and fads. As one can see, the elements that influence a purchase decision go far beyond a product's most apparent benefits. They include both quantitative and qualitative factors.

Quantitative elements have a defined value attached to them. Examples of this can include a product's price, utility, expected longevity, warranty, and resale value. They are the factors that are most often placed into a strategic campaign and touted as a reason to purchase.

For the most part, qualitative factors do not have a hard value attached to them. However, they are equal, if not more important, in finalizing any purchase decision. Qualitative factors may be defined as the components that make up a brand's value, or the perceived value that consumers attach to a product. Such elements may include connotations that a product's name carries, the position of a product with current trends, associations peer groups make with the product and with a product's design or name, and ease in communicating with the sales force.

Let's be honest. How many of us have been absolutely, positively, 100 percent sure of every purchase? The answer is most of us—especially for larger purchases—experience some hesitation. Most of us collect as much data as possible and then go with our gut feelings. Yes, each of us tries to make an educated decision, but that decision almost always relies on some very emotional responses. "Do I trust the salesperson?"

"Does it say something about who I am?" "Will my peers like it?" These are all factors in the decision-making process.

During this phase, every marketer has an opportunity to influence the purchase decision by providing more than just facts and information. By providing consultation and advice to a potential customer, almost any marketer can strongly influence the final purchase decision. Even more importantly, a marketer can create a relationship with the consumer providing them with the reassurances they seek for having made a wise purchase decision. Do not underestimate the power of this.

At this point, almost every product has brand associations that have been created from public opinion and past experiences, so the best way a salesperson can influence the buyer is by providing the customer with the information they need to finalize their purchase decision.

Purchase

In the past, purchases were completed in person. With the advent of direct mail and the telephone, purchases are increasingly made through telephone and mail orders, both of which are now booming areas of business.

Today, one of the fastest growth areas for sales is on the Internet. Examples of this have traditionally included such companies as Amazon.com and Dell Computer, but more often they include such smaller Web sites as tractor toys.com, designeroutlet.com, and tradeshop.com. Each of these businesses continues to prove consumers are willing to purchase products over the Internet, often spending from several to several thousand dollars.

At this point, the customer has made their purchase decision, and is only expecting to finalize their sale. As almost every sales manual states, the most important thing the customer wants is a reaffirmation that their decision was the right one. The most common reason a customer backs out of a sale is that the service they expect is lacking, causing them to doubt the integrity of the sale, future customer service, and even the product itself.

However, how many of us have also heard the immortal phrase, "Do you want fries with that burger?" Every sales force can, and should, try to up-sell the customer to a better product or to sell potential product add-ons. No, this does not mean adding on useless products to an existing purchase. It does mean trying to provide the customer with a component that will actually improve their experience with their purchase. This can range from asking the customer if they want fries with their burger, or suggesting they add power windows to a new car.

Most importantly, every sale opens up an opportunity to gain a customer for the future. Such things as customer clubs, ongoing mailings, and informational Web sites add value to the customer's purchase, but they will not participate in these if they don't feel good about their sale.

Developing a conversation with the customer is crucial to creating a brand-loyal buyer from that customer, and now is the time to begin. Amazon.com offers to send customers the titles of books they are interested in. Saturn has created a buyer's program that includes picnics, factory tours, and promises of ongoing customer service. Both of these companies have created programs that create consumers that can be marketed and resold for life.

Remember that it is far cheaper to sell to an existing customer than to find a new one.

Product Use/Customer Service

Every purchase carries with it an implied level of service that the customer expects to receive. Whether it is the intent of the company to provide the expected level or not is irrelevant. Today's consumer expects an increasing amount of value with their purchase in the way of continuing service. It is the company's ability to meet these expectations that influences the consumer's decision to buy from the company again.

Customer service is one of the most important phases in the sales cycle and it is often one of the most overlooked. Next to the actual performance of the product, it has the most influence over the customer's impression of the product and the company. Customer service is what creates the ongoing brand.

Customer service includes every point of communication the company has with the customer after his or her purchase. From a follow-up letter thanking the customer for their purchase, to the time in which a defective product is repaired, to the ease with which a product can be returned, customer service is what turns customers into brand loyalists, which means additional purchases for the marketer.

Whereas most marketers consider the purchase complete, it is at this stage that as much, if not more, effort needs to be made to keep the customer happy. An ongoing customer service program is needed to maintain contact and keep the conversation with the customer active.

The easiest part about customer service is that the marketer knows exactly whom they are trying to reach. The only question they need to respond to is what the message will be. This could mean creating a newsletter to provide customers with information about new products or product upgrades, telephoning a recent customer to ensure their happiness with their purchase, using direct mail to make an annual house call, or providing additional product information using an automated telephone service. All are ways to maintain a conversation with the customer and generate additional sales.

Repurchase Decision

Depending on the product, a customer may decide to add additional components (e.g., more memory to a computer), purchase a different product from the company's product line (e.g., a Gucci shirt to go with the pants), or upgrade to a newer version (e.g., a new Volkswagon Bug). Regardless of the product, the decision to repurchase is based on their experience with the given product and with the product's company through its customer service.

The process of making a repurchase is very similar to the entire sales cycle, albeit condensed. Having owned a given product, the majority of buyers know what they want and are very aware of the products being offered. The majority of their decision is whether their current product line can meet their needs or if another product would be better.

The marketer's opportunity at this point has already come and gone. As the adage goes, it is far cheaper to keep an existing customer than to close a new one. The key is customer service.

By marketing to a customer, while they are a customer, a company can elevate that person to the brand loyalist level—the point where someone believes in their brand so deeply that the product is valued beyond just its immediate benefits, and its very name begins to imply a certain lifestyle. Think of the Volkswagen Bug or the Saturn.

A company can keep in contact with the customer through newsletters, customer service programs, ongoing purchase opportunities, new product announcements and upgrades, up-coming or exclusive sales, and product participation. This not only provides the customer with more product information, it creates an ongoing conversation with the customer that positions the product foremost in the customer's mind making it the most likely product they will purchase.

Credit card companies have long been aware that cardholders are most likely to continue using the first credit card they receive, and if they can capture college students before they establish themselves in the workplace, they will continue being loyal customers well past graduation day.

THE EIGHT RULES OF EFFECTIVE ONLINE SELLING

Now that you have an overview of the sales process, it is important to understand the basic rules to marketing and selling on the Internet. They are not new. You have probably seen them before in some shape or form, and yes, they apply to offline marketing and sales as well. Regardless of your business or your product, they will help promote your online presence, drive customers to your product, and eventually close a sale.

These rules are referred to again and again. Read them, refer to them, and think how they have affected the way you buy products and how they can be applied to your customers and to your business.

Rule 1—Relationships Sell Products

Everyone is more comfortable buying from someone they know and trust. If a customer has a relationship with a salesperson, they are more likely to refer to them for information and most likely make a purchase from them. Why? Because customers do not like a lot of surprises. They want to know a brand will deliver. If it fails to deliver, they want to know someone can help them without a lot of double-talk. Almost any salesperson will tell you that creating a relationship with a customer is the most important part of selling.

This is no different for a product or a brand. If a person has used a particular product and trusts it, then they are more likely to buy it a second time. Again, customers want a product that delivers on its promises. If a consumer knows a brand will deliver (e.g., has a relationship with that brand), they are more likely to buy it again and again.

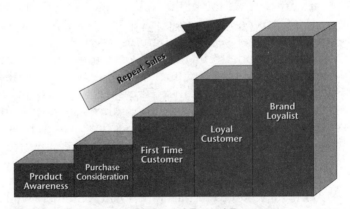

Building Business with Loyal Brand Buyers

Like any relationship, a customer/product relationship is the result of an ongoing conversation between the customer and the brand. Traditionally, this conversation begins with advertising. If a customer responds to what advertising says, they will enter a store where the conversation continues with a salesperson. If the salesperson can leverage this conversation into a relationship, they have a sale and the conversation continues with customer service and hopefully, to another sale.

When successful companies talk about moving customers along the sales process, they are talking about maintaining an ongoing conversation with that customer and building a brand relationship. When successful, it will turn consumers into customers, and customers into brand loyalists and long-term purchasers.

A brand relationship can be as simple as knowing a Coke will satisfy a thirst and reaching for it over another soda. It can be as complex as knowing you are joining an extended family when you purchase a Saturn. It should be of no surprise that the brand with the strongest customer relationship is the one most likely to succeed. The stronger the relationship when it comes time to purchase, the more likely that customer will be to buy a particular brand.

The goal of on- and offline marketing is to build awareness, create consideration, induce trial, and affect the final purchase decision. This means creating a relationship between the customer and the brand that is maintained throughout the sales cycle.

Throughout this book keep in mind how relationships are created and maintained. Selling outright does not create relationships. They are created by responding to the consumer's need for information and by providing a consistent message that the consumer will remember.

Rule 2—Selling Starts Before a Customer Walks into a Store

Many people think the sales process consists of two steps. One, driving consumers into a store through advertising, and two, selling to them by answering questions and promoting the product's benefits. But how many of us actually wait until we enter a store to make a decision?

Today's consumer rarely waits until they enter a store before developing some level of decision to purchase one brand over another. For most businesses this is one of the greatest opportunities of the Internet. By responding to the consumers' need for information and providing them with the information they are looking for earlier in the sales cycle, a business of any size can develop the kind of branded relationship that at one time only corporations with large ad budgets could afford.

Although the way individual products and services are sold differs, the basic process remains the same. The consumer identifies a need, researches potential products, considers various brands, and comes to a purchase decision.

Depending on the product being purchased and the value of that purchase, this process can take place in a matter of minutes (e.g., the purchase of a Coke over a Pepsi) or over several months and even years (e.g., the purchase of an NT server over a Sun System).

Throughout the sales cycle a number of opportunities arise where a brand can speak directly to the consumer. Not only can this start a relationship that induces them to purchase a given product but it also enables a brand to further promote that product to friends and associates through product recommendations.

Throughout the sales cycle, brand marketing positions a product in the consumer's mind by developing a personality consumers respond to (e.g., Apple was introduced as the computer for the rebel in all of us; Saturn was introduced as the "people's" car). Tactical marketing, on the other hand, provides specific consumer benefits that help the sales team sell (e.g., better interface, faster processor, more miles to the gallon). The integration of brand and tactical marketing into one campaign is the secret to successful selling. Thanks to the Internet, this now needs to occur sooner in the sales process because that is when consumers start to shop.

If you doubt this, just remember how long it took you to buy your first computer.

Rule 3—The Marketing Conversation Is Salesmanship Multiplied

John Kennedy described good advertising as "salesmanship multiplied" in his book, *Intensive Advertising*. Marketing is no different. It is a tool that can increase the effectiveness of any sales team by converting consumers into customers before they walk into a store, on or off the Internet. It does this by creating a relationship and by providing compelling benefits to which consumers respond.

We know that people are more comfortable buying a product they are familiar with. We also know they are more comfortable purchasing from someone they know and trust. Marketing is simply the tool that tells people about a product and makes them comfortable with it. Effective marketing does this well before that customer ever gets into the store. In this way, marketing acts like an advance sales team, creating a conversation with the consumer, promoting the product benefits, and supporting the brand. If successful, by the time a consumer enters a store, he or she is already a customer.

The product side of the marketing conversation combines advertising, public relations, sales, and customer service to respond to consumer concerns, close sales, and ensure the consumer is happy with the product. However, as the concept of a conversation implies, the consumer also needs a voice, and this has been conspicuously missing from traditional advertising for a long time.

While the product's side of the conversation promotes the brand and product benefits, the consumer's side of the conversation asks questions about the product, makes requests for changes and revisions, and tries to ensure the product will meet their needs. In this way, marketing acts like a preliminary sales force to tell potential customers about the benefits that a product can deliver. It also listens to the consumer to find out what they want to see in the product, translating the consumer's needs into attributes that will make them buy.

When truly effective, marketing develops an ongoing conversation that starts well before the consumer thinks of buying, and lasts well after the check clears the bank. This ongoing conversation helps to:

1. Create a product that meets the needs of the consumer (customer research);
2. Tell the consumer about the product (advertising, PR);
3. Answer the consumer's questions and concerns to close a sale (sales); and
4. Listen to the consumer to ensure the product and the service continues to meet the customer's needs (customer service, sales).

As can be seen, to be effective, marketing needs to create a conversation that lasts throughout the product development and sales cycle. It must not only promote product benefits, but also ask the consumer what they want and be able to respond to those requests.

This is one area in which the Internet surpasses all other mediums. Because of a Web site's ability to combine text and graphics to create a branded environment, and simultaneously respond to a consumer's needs, it creates a very powerful medium for creating a brand and promoting product benefits. The key to successful marketing on the Internet is to initiate and maintain a conversation with the online consumer that starts well before they decide to purchase a product and continues well after they have paid.

Rule 4—Profiting Through Targeting

It is estimated today's consumer receives over 1,500 advertising messages every day. At risk of being overwhelmed with this information, they have become very adept at shutting off the vast majority of these messages, and only focusing on those that directly affect them. At the same time, today's consumer is more wary of advertising than ever before. They understand the advertising process and know that advertising is meant to sell products. Because of this, they are less trustful of the message being delivered.

Just as important, today's consumers have realized their value as purchasers, and are less afraid to ask for a product that fits their individual needs. They do not want a cure-all, because they know from experience a jack-of-all-trades product is rarely the master they are seeking.

This means today's consumer no longer wants laundry detergent. They want Tide with extra whitener, or Tide Ultra for tough stains or softer clothes. Yes, consumers are brand driven, but unless that brand responds to their specific needs with very specific benefits, they will try new products they feel fit their individual needs.

In order to break through the ad clutter and respond to the consumer's need for a more personal product, manufacturers, almost regardless of the category, are introducing products that specifically target a consumer's need—and, in order not to miss an opportunity, they are doing it at a faster pace than ever before. This is not expected to slow down in any foreseeable future, for without this, they risk being lost in the clutter and passed over by the consumer.

Creating a well-defined product for a targeted audience builds an effective and efficient business. In doing so, a company may lose some of the overall market, but they will attract their primary audience quicker and establish themselves in the market earlier. Remember, today's consumer does not want something that is made for everyone; they want a product they can call their own.

Regardless of whether you are promoting a product or a Web site on the Internet, the same holds true. On the Internet consumers can find information on just about any subject they can imagine. For a business, this produces endless opportunities and an equal amount of traps. When a consumer is looking for information on a subject or a particular product, they look for it in a very specific category.

Unless a Web site focuses on one very specific niche, it will never attract the consumer you are trying to reach. It's far too easy to spend precious time and resources creating a Web site that promotes too many things. As you will see, focusing on one identifiable product and brand is the first step to success on the Internet.

Rule 5—One Product, One Message

As with any relationship, the consumer/product relationship is strengthened through ongoing communication. However, unless that communication delivers a consistent message, the product risks confusing the consumer. Think of your initial reaction to an ad that says "Top of the Line Products at Rock Bottom Prices." Your most likely response to a campaign promoting low cost and high quality is distrust. The reason for this is simple. It presents the consumer with conflicting messages that invariably tell them to look elsewhere for either a high quality product or one that is low in cost.

It is no surprise that consumers want to be sure of their purchase. Everyone wants to maximize their satisfaction and minimize their risk regardless of the product. To do this means finding a product that promotes readily identifiable benefits that meet one's needs. The only way for a product to accomplish this is through a consistent message that reflects one product, one brand, and one set of benefits.

Similar to creating a niche product for a targeted audience, delivering one message to the customer means defining what you are selling. Although this sounds easy, it is probably one of the most difficult parts of building a business.

Because the consumer rarely differentiates where they saw a particular message (e.g., television, radio, or print), today's business needs to ensure that all components of a campaign follow a consistent direction.

On the Internet it is even more important to follow this logic. With so many Web sites competing for an audience, and with so many elements being combined, it is far too easy to send a conflicting message. From text to design to video to audio, it is more important than ever to develop and maintain a branded environment that consistently reflects one look, one feel, and one voice for your product. To accomplish this is to create an online marketing and sales tool that simply cannot be outdone by any traditional medium.

Rule 6—Two-Way Communication Builds Relationships

The basis of traditional advertising is to send a series of messages to the consumer with the hope they will respond by purchasing a given product. By combining different advertising mediums into a single campaign that supports a consistent message, advertisers can hope to create a level of awareness in the consumer's mind and position themselves as the best product to buy.

The problem with this model is it's a one-way conversation. Without knowing what a particular consumer wants, an advertiser must send out a series of ads that promote slightly different benefits, with the hope that an ad pushes the right button at the right time. At the same time, the only way for the consumer to have their questions answered is to pick up a telephone or walk into a store. By the time that occurs, they have already made a number of decisions without your help.

Like any one-sided conversation, a one-sided conversation between the product and the customer falls far short of effective communication and is probably not the most efficient use of time and money. Being able to listen to a consumer's concerns earlier in the sales process allows a company to respond to them before their competition can, and this is an opportunity to sell before anyone else can.

Throughout the sales cycle, consumers look for information. The company that responds to this need is the company that can create a relationship, not just by throwing out a consistent message, but by finding out what the consumers' needs are and by responding to them. Providing the information they seek will result in being the one most will turn to when it comes time to make a purchase.

Only through two-way communication can such a relationship be created, and today the most effective and efficient way to do this is through the Internet.

Rule 7—Consumers, Not Web Sites, Own the Internet

Consumers use the World Wide Web to search for information. Most have a specific product in mind and are looking for information to help them solidify their purchase decision. Yes, they will probably investigate several brands, but they will also look for new products and brands to ensure they have all the facts. It should be of no surprise that those Web sites that provide the best information are the ones consumers will most likely visit.

Because of this, the Internet has become one of the most user-driven mediums around. With the click of a mouse, the consumer has total control over which Web sites they visit and what content they see. With thousands of choices, if a particular Web site does not provide them with the information or entertainment they are seeking, they will go to another site with the click of a mouse.

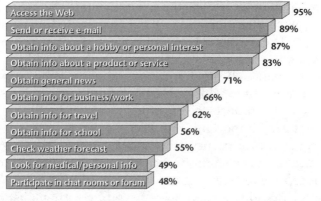

Source: Intelliquest,1Q 1990

What People Are Doing Online

For the marketer, this means that trying to draw a consumer in with flashy advertising will not be enough to keep them. The online advertiser must actually work to understand what the consumer wants to be able to respond appropriately. This also means as soon as a consumer enters a given Web site he or she has pre-qualified himself or herself as a potential customer. By merely clicking on a mouse, they have demonstrated some level of interest in a given product or category. At this point, as the saying goes, it is up to the advertiser to lose the sale.

Without constantly responding to the consumer's requests and maintaining the consumer's interest, they risk losing them to another Web site and another product.

Rule 8—On the Internet, Content Is King

The television audience rarely cares what network they tune into; they do, however, care about the program they watch. They identify with the characters and the plot of a given show—the network's content.

This is no different on the Internet. People visit a Web site because it is able to provide them with the information or entertainment they seek. People care less about the network that provides it; they care about the ease and accuracy of the content. With this in mind, the goal of an online business is not to drive consumers to a company's Web site. The goal is to get the consumer to its branded content.

Like a live salesperson, the Internet allows the advertiser to do more than just deliver a slogan or static advertisement. It allows the advertiser to say, "We know what you want, and we can deliver it." The content is what initially attracts the consumer. It is also what will maintain the consumer's attention and will entice them to buy again and again.

The creation of content is the first step in promoting a product or developing a marketing campaign on the World Wide Web. Content does not mean Web site. It means producing some type of information or entertainment to which a particular audience will respond.

The importance of content is also why the creation of branded content is so important. Branded content is online content that reflects the benefits of a particular brand. It enables the marketer to deliver their message in an environment where the consumer is comfortable and more receptive to receiving it.

Branded content goes beyond creating a list of product features. It goes beyond creating a sales pitch for a given product. Effective branded content means providing the consumer with the information they are seeking without obviously biasing it toward a particular brand. No, branded content is not an ad. It is information the consumer wants to receive. When poorly constructed, the consumer is reminded of a shill. When well crafted, the consumer says, "I know this is brought to me by brand X, but it is useful information that I wanted to see."

Yes, developing and maintaining branded content takes more work than creating a banner ad, but as you will see, it is also a much more effective and efficient way to market on the Internet. Because content is what drives the consumer, the creation and management of content will continue to be of increasing importance to establishing a brand and building a business online.

Ask any successful online marketer and they will tell you they are more online publisher than strict advertiser.

WHY THE WEB?

This section was created for today's marketing executive who is trying to determine if they should bring their product onto the Internet. If you already know that the Internet is the place for you to build your business, you may want to skim over this section. It does provide good information and will help you focus your online efforts, but an in-depth read is probably not necessary.

However, if you have questions, or if your boss questions why you should be moving your business onto the Internet, this section was created to help you make a decision and support it.

Regardless, this section is not an argument for moving all your advertising dollars away from print or television or radio and onto the Internet. It is an argument for augmenting your offline advertising efforts with an online component.

Traditional Advertising—An Inefficient Way to Close a Sale

The basis of traditional advertising is to target a specific consumer audience. Then send them a consistent advertising message with as much frequency as a budget will allow. If successful, the consumer will respond when it comes time to make their purchase decision. Although this gets the word to the consumer audience, it fails to develop a relationship that will sell without spending a lot of money.

There is no way to know where in the sales cycle the consumer is, which means the marketer's message may or may not address their immediate concerns. Without having their concerns and questions answered, the average consumer has little reason to pursue a given product. This means traditional advertising fails in a crucial component of closing a sale—responding to the individual needs of the consumer.

Just as important, traditional advertising is inefficient in measuring its effectiveness. Yes, an advertiser can measure reach and frequency to assess how many people are potentially seeing a product's message. However, these are measurement devices that have always been in great question. Advertisers pay according to the estimated number of people who will see an advertised message. However, viewers change channels during commercials or leave the television set altogether; readers often skim over advertisements in magazines or newspapers; and listeners are known to change the channel when their music is interrupted. So, the ability to assess exactly how many have seen or heard a particular ad is very subjective and dependent on the ad's ability to attract the consumer's eye or ear, not necessarily an element of the medium's ability to deliver an audience.

We do not doubt that advertising works. The fact that people remember jingles and ad campaigns years after they have run is proof that they work. However, there are questions as to whether traditional advertising is the only, or the most, effective way to reach an intended audience and create a relationship that sells.

This is where the Internet comes into play. By enhancing proven brand concepts with the interactive nature of new media technology, today's marketer can at last create a brand-driven relationship based on a two-way conversation that is driven by the consumer. If the online capability to create relationships is combined with the offline ability to reach a mass audience, this two-way conversation can build lasting relationships. However, the refusal to incorporate online advertising is a sure way to maintain a one-way conversation that will lose the consumer once they begin looking online.

An Attractive Audience in a Growing Mass Medium

Today, the Internet is able to deliver a very targeted audience based on content or demographics. As the Internet continues to grow, it will be even better able to target a specific consumer. The advantage is, as the Internet becomes more accessible to the general market through the introduction of less expensive computers and more consumer-friendly interfaces such as WebTV, it will be able to deliver a greater variety of consumers and a larger number of consumers within each niche.

What does this mean for advertisers and marketers? It means being able to reach a mass audience while still being able to deliver to a specific customer depending on the goals of the advertiser.

Today the primary problem advertisers find with the Internet is its inability to deliver the mass audience that television or print can reach.[1] However, as the Internet continues to grow it will be able to draw that audience from a pool of consumers that reaches around the world.

The secret to using the Internet effectively is to create a long-term marketing plan that promotes a consistent brand message. Today, work on targeting a specific consumer through content and other means. As the Internet continues to grow, this marketing plan can take advantage of growing technologies to target a specific consumer within the growing mass audience.

However, by delaying entry today the cautious advertiser risks missing out on establishing themselves when the medium is young, resulting in paying a higher entry price when the medium matures.

Brand and Tactical Marketing with Sales Capabilities

Television, print, radio, outdoor—businesses have been trying to get their hands around exactly what the World Wide Web is. When television

---

[1]Appendix 2 contains online resources with up-to-date consumer demographics.

was introduced, programming tried to emulate radio and then stage productions, and efforts at advertising were not much different. It took years until people finally realized how to use the new medium.

The Web is no different. It is like no other medium we have seen. Much like a television commercial, a Web site is able to project a product's brand in the overall look and feel of the content. Similar to print, the Internet is an inexpensive way to deliver a very detailed rationale behind the benefits of a product. Like direct mail, the use of online databases allows businesses to target specific consumers and address their perceived needs. However, unlike any of these mediums, the Internet allows advertisers to create real-time conversations, in which consumers can ask questions before they purchase. More importantly, they can have those questions answered by the advertiser. This creates a seamless flow of information that is immediate and brings the consumer directly into the marketing process regardless of where they are in the sales cycle.

Because of the World Wide Web's ability to create a branded environment in which to promote products and conduct sales, it is unique among other marketing mediums. The only other element in the sales process able to do this is an actual store, and, like a store, the best way to benefit through the Internet is to create a brand-driven campaign that produces bottom line results.

So, how do today's businesses do this? The answer—create online content that consumers will respond to by providing them with the information they seek, and promote it. Just look at television commercials. They are no longer the bland product pitches of the '70s. They are 30-second story lines with enough special effects to dazzle someone into watching. This is no different when creating an online presence.

Regardless of the immediate goals, the key to the Internet is the content. Content is what drives consumers to a given Web site. Content holds the advertiser's message. Content is what enables the advertiser to initiate and develop a relationship with the consumer to which the consumer will respond.

Advantages of Web Marketing Throughout the Sales Cycle

Online Marketing Benefits

Any Web-based marketing effort combines some other form of online content (e.g., a Web site), with online advertising. Like offline advertising, online advertising not only drives consumers to a particular site, but helps to pre-qualify consumers based on their interests. For example, banner advertising is a way to grab consumers based on their interests and drive them to a Web site. The Web site is the branded element that enables a company to communicate with and respond to the concerns of its customers enabling them to sell.

What makes this more effective than advertising and selling offline? Because the entire process occurs on a closed system (the Internet), it allows the marketer to control and monitor the entire customer process from qualifying customers to closing a sale. Throughout this process, marketers can track what works and what does not. Most important, today's Web marketer can adapt to changing market conditions quickly and inexpensively without knocking down a single wall.

The most valuable benefits to marketing a product online include direct customer interaction and the ability to monitor quantifiable results:

Interaction

For marketers and advertisers the most important aspect of the World Wide Web is the ability to interact directly with consumers. No other medium allows for instantaneous two-way communication. Whether this means enabling consumers to ask questions using email, or directly contacting sales help via chat, the Internet allows marketers to talk to and address the immediate concerns of consumers turning consumers into customers, and customers into brand loyalists.

Quantifiable Results

With the World Wide Web a marketer can track almost any Web-based activity. Online marketers can monitor traffic on a Web site or the response rate of a banner ad continuously and automatically. Almost instantaneously marketers can measure the success of a given program from start to finish and make adjustments accordingly. Being able to quantify results also means measuring the true effect of marketing dollars. Unlike television, radio, or print, advertisers know exactly how many eyes have seen and responded to a specific ad and adjust accordingly.

Self-Qualifying Content

Because consumers select the content they see, they qualify themselves as interested consumers according to their needs. This means the marketing message can be tailored to address a specific phase in the sales cycle, and respond to perceived needs that commonly arise during that phase. In addition, it also provides the ability to determine where in the sales cycle a product is losing potential sales.

Inexpensive

Unlike print or television, once a Web site has been created, changing, updating, and revising its content to meet market trends is easy and inexpensive. It doesn't require the level of production other mediums demand, and with technology advancing at an increasing pace, Web sites will continue to be easier and less expensive to create and maintain in the future.

Flexible

Imagine knowing how many people actually saw a television commercial, and how many actually responded to it. With this information, an advertiser could revise the commercial to ensure it induced the best reaction from the audience. With online advertising, marketers can continually test and change their advertising to ensure they maintain the best response rate possible.

Benefits of Online Content

A well-designed Web site is the cornerstone of any online marketing effort. However, it is not the only way to promote on the Internet. Online content is what provides consumers with the information they are seeking and enables a company to truly brand its product or service. Some of what online content can do includes:

Branding

Well-designed online content allows marketers to truly brand their product. A Web site, for example, is a place where every aspect of the consumer environment is controlled by the marketer, much like the way Disney controls the look and feel of their retail stores. With this in mind, an online presence can be created that combines graphics, text, sounds, and even video that support a specific brand. With the Web as a tool, a savvy marketer can create a truly branded environment with which to approach consumers and convert them into customers.

Product Information

Creating ten pages of product information takes no more time than entering the text into a word processor. Providing ample information to the consumer, as detailed or as general as the company allows, is easy. Changing that information as the product advances is just as easy. No other medium allows such a quick and inexpensive way to disseminate information than the Internet.

Sales Leads

Today's marketers are not just promoting products on the Web. They are generating and closing transactions. Today, companies can take customers from shopping to purchasing without ever having to open a door. If there is any doubt about the profits that can be made, take a look at some of the case studies in this book.

Sales Team

In today's global and highly competitive market, sales teams need a tactical advantage over competitors. A Web site can provide just that. Sales presentations and information can be placed on a protected Web site for access anywhere in the world, 24 hours a day. Any sales team can be better equipped to provide sales sheets, product information, even live demonstrations as clients request them on the spot—and that gives them an advantage in closing a sale.

Customer Service

Imagine a customer contacting a company any time of the day, any day of the week. With a Web site, customers can have questions answered, receive detailed product information, even have issues brought to their attention without ever having to involve the customer service staff. By creating a fully interactive customer service area, complete with answers to common questions, not only can customer problems and requests be addressed, but marketing information can be gathered without ever making a customer feel put out.

Online Advertising Benefits

Online advertising is the primary method to drive traffic to online content. It allows marketers to target custom messages to niche audiences. Each message directs the recipient to content that responds to their specific needs. By planning a targeted campaign, online advertising can be a very effective tool in selecting, qualifying, and converting consumers into customers.

Online advertising combines the benefits of brand, tactical, even direct response advertising within one medium. Regardless of which tool is employed (e.g., banners, content, email) advertisers can easily:

1. Monitor exactly how many eyes have seen a given message;
2. Target customers with customized messages based on demographics or content; and
3. Pre-qualify customers before they visit based on their interest level.

Additional benefits of online advertising include:

Targetable

Advertisers are not only able to control who sees their ads, but they control when and where they are seen with greater precision than with any other medium. Online advertising can target specific users based on page content, demographics, even psychographics. Advertisers can approach a specific audience in an environment the consumer chooses, and deliver a customized message that produces results.

Measurable

Every time a banner ad is "served" to a user's computer, it is counted. Each count is monitored and reported so advertisers know exactly how many consumers have not only seen, but responded to it. No other medium—television, radio, or print—can offer this level of tracking. With this information, marketers know instantly what ads are effective to ensure the most efficient and effective ads are maintained.

Actionable

Online advertising combines the best possible scenario to generate responses. Regardless of what medium is being used, some response mechanism can be built in. Banner ads can link directly to a catalog where someone can order a product with the click of a button. There is no dialing a phone, no completing a response card, just a direct connection to an online cash register. With a tap of a mouse button, one prequalified consumer becomes a customer.

Going Online in Brief

Almost anything a consumer could want is available somewhere on the Internet. This is its power. It is also its trap. Too many online businesses allow themselves to stray from their objectives. They try to deliver everything to the customers, becoming jacks-of-all-trades, and masters of none.

Running a successful online business means going back to the basics. This means identifying an objective, developing a focused strategy to reach that objective, and creating a systematic plan to implement that strategy. It is not as difficult as it sounds. The real trick is keeping the plan flexible, assessing how well the plan works, and shifting the plan to meet consumer needs.

There are four basic steps to developing any successful online business. They include:

Step 1—Build Content

Develop online content that provides useful information to the consumer. Online consumers are looking for information. It's one of the top reasons anyone is on the Web. This does not mean a Web site has to include every byte of information about a product, but it does mean providing enough information to start a relationship with consumers. The risk is spending too much time putting up extraneous information. Thus, the more targeted and consumer-oriented the content, the more effective will be the Web site.

Step 2—Drive Traffic

Think of a Web site as a store. Consumers may see it while driving by but unless they know what's inside, chances are they will not stop in. Promoting a Web site is more than just running a banner ad. It means creating a campaign that combines banner ads, sweepstakes, and lots of links with other sites. It means taking your Web site's content off the URL and onto the Internet. A Web site must not only be advertised, it must be expanded.

Step 3—Listen to the Customer

If an advertiser does not know what a customer wants, they lose them to someone who does. Knowing what a customer wants means asking them and then listening to what they have to say. On the World Wide Web, businesses can accomplish this with the benefits of having a cash register just a click away. The trick is to provide the customers some mechanism to talk. Believe me, they will if given the opportunity, but once they do, you'd better listen.

Step 4—Use the Web as a First Line for Sales

When consumers enter a store, they usually want information. Online consumers are no different. Provide online consumers with the information they want and they will read it. Just don't forget to give them an opportunity to actually make a purchase. This means providing them with ways to receive more information or to make a purchase. Either way, by creating content that helps users learn about and sample products, an ongoing conversation can be developed that will turn consumers into customers. Just make sure you provide them with a way to buy.

CONCLUSION

Like any marketing effort, all online advertising should leverage the established brand. Yes, advertising online needs to keep the particulars of the Internet in mind, but having to create an entirely new campaign just for the Internet would be like developing new and independent campaigns for television, radio, and print. This is not a very good way to establish a brand, but an excellent waste of advertising dollars.

Like any advertising, the campaign comes first and the creative comes second, and, as an effective television campaign can be extended into print and radio, so too can a print, television, or radio campaign be extended onto the Web. With the Web, it just needs to be taken a step further.

The Web allows marketers to take a slogan and put it into action. Rather than just saying "we understand the customer," on the Web marketers can prove it by asking customers what they want, and delivering it. Whether this means creating an online customer service area or allowing customers to voice compliments, complaints, even ideas for improvements, marketers can listen to what the customer is asking for and respond.

For years marketers have been trying to create relationships with consumers and customers. Now, that opportunity exists. The next question is how quickly will businesses use it.

CHAPTER TWO

The First Step to Going Online: Developing a Brand

This chapter is all about doing research and making lists. I admit it is not the glamorous part of building an online business, but it is essential to creating a successful one.

This chapter is designed to help you define your product, your brand, your category, and your customer. Without this information you may as well triple your budget and reduce your goals by half. Without this information, you will not be able to create an online presence to which your customers will respond.

Too many people start by convincing themselves they know their product and their customer. They next move forward and design a Web site or hire a company to do it for them. Then half-way through the design process they begin to see what their competition is doing or what their customer is asking for, and begin to revise their plans accordingly. Not a big problem until the invoice arrives. Don't make this mistake or you will pay for it in money, time, or both.

Remember the Internet is very different than the real world. Things that work offline do not work online and vice versa. Do the homework. Explore what others are doing. Find out who is doing it right and who is doing it wrong. You will pay one way or the other. By doing the research up front, you will simply pay less and save a great deal of time. More importantly, your customer will see a much better product without being bothered with a constantly changing design.

This chapter will walk you though some basic research you should do before creating any kind of an Internet presence.

DEFINING THE PRODUCT AND THE AUDIENCE TO SELL

The process for starting a business online is no different than starting a business anywhere. It means creating a dependable product or service that people will rely on. It means developing a name people will remember. Above all, it means creating a relationship with customers that will bring them back again and again. In simple terms, it means creating a product and a brand to which people respond; then it means refining that brand to meet the needs of the customer.

What is the brand? One textbook describes a brand as "the name and associations the consumer affixes to a given product or service." In real terms, the brand is the personality of the product you are selling. If your product were a person, think of the brand as their personality.

As we have seen, consumers go through a process when they consider buying a product. They first ask themselves, "Will this product meet my basic needs?" For those products that meet their basic needs, consumers begin to look at other quantifiable benefits a given product will provide.

Assuming that your product is something people actually want or need, consumers begin to place a great deal of value on the brand cachet the product will provide. At this point, it becomes easier to promote a product in terms of brand rather than just product benefits, because it is

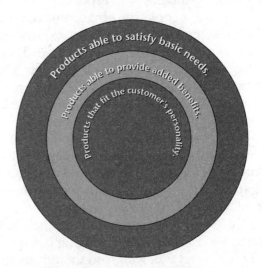

How the Brand Affects the Consumer's
Purchase Decision

easier for the consumer to visualize the product and make the necessary associations that will lead to a purchase.

Is the product reliable? Is it exciting? Is it extravagant? Nobody knows your product better than you do, and the process of developing a brand that consumers respond to is the key to getting consumers to know your product.

Building a Consumer Relationship by Building a Brand

When a product creates an identifiable personality, it is taking the first step to building an ongoing relationship with its customers. In today's market, regardless of the product, this is increasingly essential to keeping existing customers.

Without developing some level of trust with customers, and without responding to customer's concerns and needs, almost any company risks losing them to the competitor most willing to do so. Without a relationship that consumers can rely on, there is little reason for them to repurchase a given product. There are simply too many choices available, and more are entering the market every day.

Saturn, the auto manufacturer, is an example of a company that understands the value of building a customer-driven relationship. Before it built its first car, Saturn identified key elements consumers felt were missing in the automotive industry.

Saturn identified two issues customers had with the current automotive industry. Interestingly, they did not deal with the cars, but with the selling process. First was the customer's dread of haggling with the proverbial car salesman. Second, customers were willing to forego some luxuries in order to afford a car that met their transportation needs. By creating a product and company that responded to the customer, they were able to quickly enter and create a foothold in the highly competitive automotive market.

This is not a fluke incidence. Almost 20 years before, a company called Honda did this with the Accord. Twenty years before that, a company called Volkswagen did the same thing with the Beetle. In all of these instances, a company identified and responded to the consumer's needs. Not only did they sell cars, they created a customer-driven relationship, a relationship that has endeared them to the Volkswagen Beetle and Honda Accord for years after that initial campaign.

So, how do you take the lessons learned by Saturn to drive your business? By listening to the customer and building a brand that responds to their needs.

Creating a Brand-Driven Campaign by Defining the Product

Every product has a personality. It is based on more than just product benefits, but on the same intangibles that reflect a person's personality. Consumers associate specific images with a product based on the advertising they see; on past experiences they have had with the product and its company; on information they gather; on recommendations made to them; even on associations made with the product's name. Regardless of whether a company promotes this image or allows the consumer to create his or her own impression, it will exist. And like any human, it is far better that a product manage its own image than allow an image to be created for it.

This image is the product's brand. Technically, a brand is simply the name given to a product or trademark. However, in advertising the brand represents everything associated with a given product.

A product's benefits will define where the product fits into a specific category based on demographics (a target age group), product applications (a faster computer chip), or an identifiable consumer need (affordable transportation). However, a brand will define that product within that niche.

Many products exist in every category, no matter how specific that category is. To compete, each product must have something that separates it from the competition. Product benefits are rarely enough to do this alone. There is simply too much competition for one product to shine on all accounts. What will help to raise one product over its competition in the mind of the consumer is the brand. Without this, the consumer has no reason to switch from their existing product or to refrain from trying another.

When Pepsi entered the cola category, Coca-Cola owned the category. Taste alone was not enough to secure their business. However, image was. Pepsi identified a younger niche market that did not identify with Coke. They viewed Coke as the soft drink of an older generation. By positioning itself with the adolescent market, Pepsi was able to carve out a niche that Coca-Cola overlooked. In this way Pepsi was able to define its brand and create an opportunity within an otherwise closed market.

Remember, product benefits help define the category in which the product competes. A brand is what defines the product itself. Together they create and define the market within which the product is sold.

The goal of creating and promoting a specific brand is to create one look, one feel, and one image with which the consumer can identify. Without this, it is too easy for the consumer to confuse what the product will do for them. Even more, it risks the consumer creating a perception of the product that may not be consistent with the product's benefits.

In creating an effective brand, almost any product will realize significant benefits. Some of these include:

- A consistent image consumers identify with and respond to, helping a product break through the advertising clutter
- An image the consumer will remember when it comes time to buy
- An increased effectiveness in advertising by better retention of the advertising message from medium to medium
- The ability to maintain a defined, targeted approach to reaching consumers
- A foundation for all corporate and product strategies

Strategy

Although each element is described in detail, the overriding processes for developing and leveraging a brand are:

1. Selecting a very targeted consumer for whom the product benefits are most important (the primary audience).
2. Identifying the benefits and aspects of the product that are most important to the primary audience.
3. Using those benefits to create a personality to which the audience will respond.
4. Leveraging that personality into a consistent image that will permeate all aspects of corporate communication.[2]

START WITH THE PROSPECT, NOT THE PRODUCT

I apologize for being the one to point this out, but in today's market there are almost no products alone in their market and without competition. For those with competition, this section is designed to help you find what other products are out there, assess how they will compete against your product,

---

[2] If you want more information on the importance of positioning a product and its impact on a product, I suggest the book, *Positioning: The Battle for Your Mind*, written by Al Ries and Jack Trout, Warner Brothers, 1981.

and help you grab a niche that your product can own. For those who feel they have none, this chapter may make you rethink where you are.

Researching Your Competition Online

Nobody knows your product better than you do. You know its benefits. You know its failures. Now is the time to put this knowledge to use by looking for its competition.

The first step is to go to any of the major directories and search engines and begin a keyword search. To do this, simply select any of the major search engines and enter your product's name. Continue doing this with each of your product's strengths and weaknesses. Each directory or search engine will provide you with a list of Web sites. These sites are your online competition.

Start with Yahoo! and continue through Altavista, Excite, and Lycos. Although you can continue with other directories, you will probably find more than enough examples of your competition in the primary directories.[3]

Next, create a spreadsheet or table similar to the one shown on page 33. The top should be a list of all the major benefits of your product. The first column should be a list of each Web site with its URL. The next columns should allow you to rate the sites based on their overall content, design, and navigation. As you continue across, list each of your product's benefits, and rate each site on how well its product competes against yours.

If I were creating an online publication for cooks, I would begin a search using such keywords as "cook," "recipes," "meals," "food," or any other related words. Depending on what is returned, the first several columns for a competitive chart might look like the figure shown.

The objectives of this exercise are to:

1. Benchmark your competition to assess what you are up against, both in content and design.
2. Evaluate how well your product or service is able to compete and determine what changes would make it do better.
3. Create a database of your competition that can be maintained to ensure you stay ahead of them in the coming months and years.

Remember, the idea is to provide yourself with an overview of what else is out there, what types of content they are providing, and how well their

---

[3] A list of search engines and directories follows in appendix 1.

Marketing Calendar

	Overall Quality	Overall Design	Overall Content	Overall Navigation	Searchable Recipes	E-mailable Recipes	Type of Recipes	Chef Interviews
Food Site #1	5 basic listings	Simple, without use of java or shock	Good, lacks content for the gourmet	Simple and easy, at the cost of design	Yes	No	Basic recipes	None
Food Site #2	Nice design, nothing that stands out	Simple and utilitarian	Good breadth of content, primarily for recipe lists	Simple and easy, appeals to all browsers	Yes, very complete by multiple categories	Yes	Historical recipes from Gourmet and Cuisine Magazine	Monthly
Food Site #3	More like a magazine than a website	Excellent design, eye catching	Great breadth of content, from recipes to regional stores & chef interviews	More user friendly than the others	Very complete appeals to the gourmet	Yes	Recipes from a variety of sources including submitted	Weekly

Competitive Site Comparison

sites are designed and maintained. This is the time to decide if there are serious competitors, or if the market is still open. A good hint should be the sheer number of Web sites you consider competition.

If you think the market is crowded, but are convinced you can stand out in a crowded market, just think about the lessons learned in the cable industry and how many channels have fallen by the wayside.

How Good Is Your Competition?

The next step in assessing your competition is to find their Achilles heels. Go through your list and see where they fall short. Sign up for their newsletters. Email them and test their customer service. Order a product and see how long it takes for it to be delivered. Call them and ask how their traffic is growing. Ask how their sales have been.[4]

People take a lot of pride in their Web sites, and are often very willing to talk about them if they are asked in the right way. The information you find out will be invaluable in avoiding their mistakes. It's far cheaper to make a Web site correctly by learning from the mistakes of the competition than in having to fix those mistakes later on.

You may be surprised to find some very obvious opportunities that you can turn into an advantage. Is their content old? Do their products respond to a consumer need? Take a look at the brand personality you

---

[4] An excellent tool to rate Web sites can be found at *www.websitegarage.com*. Although this is a pay service, they have created a free component where Web Garage performs a quick site review on any URL entered. This covers technical, design, and navigation aspects.

developed. What elements have existing Web sites missed? What elements do they do well? The Internet is far too big a place for any one Web site to have all the answers, and that is where your opportunity lies. Your goal is to determine which elements are important to your consumers and find the gaps where the elements are missing.

Returning to the cooking Web site example. If you are creating a Web site for gourmet chefs, where does Epicurious.com fall short? What service are they missing that you can provide? Perhaps you should add a way for customers to rank recipes, or maybe chat with star chefs. Is it a tie-in to a television program or magazine to boost the overall reach? The answer is yes to each, depending on what you are trying to achieve.

Don't think for a minute that Barnes & Noble just built their Web site without doing a very complete analysis of Amazon.com and learning from their mistakes.

Is Your Audience on the Net? If So, Who Are They?

Have you ever noticed there is a Burger King near every McDonald's? Years ago, one of those companies spent millions of dollars researching the optimum locations for their restaurants. What did the other one do? They waited to see where their competition built a restaurant and built one across the street. Why do the research twice if the results are already available?

We all know the Internet is one of the fastest growing communications mediums around. We have all seen the reports of how it is overtaking television, but is your customer online? If so, where are they?

Again, you know your audience better than anyone else. What we want to find out is a) where is your audience going and b) who is the actual customer and what are their habits.

Once again, start with the competitive Web sites you already identified. Revisit them and look for secondary content and link pages. Both will provide insight into who your customer is and what they look for online. Begin by writing down the trends you find. Create a list of these elements in order to construct a profile of your customer. If you think you already know them, you may be surprised by what you find.

Yes, some of this data will be questionable, so use common sense. However, if a consistent trend emerges that goes against your "gut" feeling, make a note of it, but do not rule it out completely. I do not know of one site that has not been surprised by the customers it attracts.

Additionally, as your site grows advertisers, investors will want this information. It is important to have comparative data if you do not yet have data of your own.

The goal of this exercise is to make a list of your consumer's attributes in one customer review. This review should include all the demographic and psychographic information you can gather, including the habits, likes, and dislikes that represent your average visitor.[5]

Secondary Content

In an attempt to provide information to their visitors, many sites will include secondary information that is of interest to its audience. For example, a Web site for gourmands may include travel information because people who enjoy good food often enjoy travel, or a Web site for books may also sell videotapes or CDs because they have found book lovers also purchase music and videotapes. Like the example of McDonald's and Burger King, your competition has probably already done your homework in identifying who your consumer is. All you need to do is research the information they have collected.

Link Pages

Another excellent source of information is link pages. Many sites will provide links to Web sites that provide secondary information to their readers. Again, follow these links, make notes of any trends you begin to see, especially what products are being advertised. Advertisers know who their audience is and what they are seeking. Many will do your work for you.

Demographics

In an effort to sell advertising, many sites include demographic information about their users. Visit the advertising information pages and make a note of ages, gender, and education levels. You will be able to see trends within this information, even if it reaffirms what you already know.

At the end of this exercise, you should know two things:

1. Who your competition is
2. Who your customer is

If you do not know this, go back and redo this exercise. Moving forward without this is like going into a battle without knowing how many

---

[5] See appendix 5 for a sample online consumer review. Although you do not need to go into this detail, any information will help you create your Web site and tailor your product and pitch to sell better.

people you are fighting and what kind of terrain you are entering. You will quickly find yourself spending more money redesigning your site and even revising your product to keep up with your competition and your customer.

Identify and Compare Consumer Benefits

If you can afford to conduct focus groups, you can probably pass over this section. If not, this is a simple process to determine how well you stack up against your competition and where you stand in the customer's eye.

On a piece of paper or using a spreadsheet, create a series of columns. In the first column, make a list of all the benefits consumers expect to receive from your product or in the products of your competitors. List them in order of importance to the consumer. In the second column, list your product. In the remaining columns, add each of your competitors' products. Now, rank each consumer benefit according to how well you, and each of your competitors, are able to deliver on them. Use a scale from 1 to 5. Such benefits should include price, dependability, value, color, physical appearance, brand recognition, and ease of use.

Repeat this process on a second spreadsheet, only this time, write down all the intangible or brand attributes associated with your product. This includes all the "cool" factors that consumers identify with your product, your brand, or your company. Now do the same thing with your competition in each of the following columns.

With this information consider all the benefits of your competition. Highlight the benefits that you and your competition share, and note where your competition is able to deliver on a benefit you lack. For the benefits that you share, determine where you surpass your competition and where your competition surpasses you. Be honest because in a very short time your customers will be brutally honest in the way they spend their time and their money.

This is the time to consider which of your product benefits are truly important to the consumer and which are not. This is also the time to consider which benefits are going to attract your key customer (your primary benefits), and which are secondary and tertiary benefits. The important part of this exercise is determining who your target customers are, what they are looking for, and which of your competition is best able to deliver those benefits to the customers.

At this stage, forget about trying to target all of the customers in your category. If you try to, you will most likely waste your resources trying to reach a secondary customer who may or may not respond to your product offering. For example, if you were trying to sell a compact vacuum cleaner designed for an apartment dweller it would be a waste of money to buy advertising targeting the general vacuum market. A good portion of your ad dollars would be spent on people who want a larger or industrial vacuum cleaner and have no intention of buying a compact unit. Instead, if you spend your money focusing on those consumers actively looking for a compact machine, 100 percent of your ad dollars will go toward the consumer most likely to buy. Once you capture your primary customer and establish a revenue stream, then you can expand your efforts to attract a wider audience. If you try too soon, you will probably be spending valuable resources on an audience that may not respond.

The spreadsheets you have created will show you the opportunities for your Web site and your product. Based on your analysis, you will be able to determine a path that carves out a niche that your competition has not covered.

At the same time, try to identify the key design elements of your competition's Web sites. Look at what works for them and what does not. The strengths of your online product will be reflected in its packaging, which means Web design.

This process is very similar to the branding process of the last chapter because that is what we are doing at this point: Determining how your online brand will be portrayed.

For products that already exist, we are not creating a new brand. We are merely considering what elements of the brand will be important to the online consumer, and which of those elements should be promoted first.

This is not a novel idea. If you look at a Coca-Cola ad on television, it portrays the lifestyle Coke represents. If you look at an in-store ad, it will promote price. Same brand, different message depending on where the consumer is in the buying process and what they are most concerned with.

Building a Brand that Sells Your Audience, Not Your Product

The moment a consumer enters a store they know somebody is going to try to sell them something. They are ready for it and are expecting a pitch. The same holds true on the Internet, only the store is now a Web site. The moment they click onto a new site, that consumer is looking for signs of how that site is going to sell them. Buttons, flashy banners, offers of low prices are all trying to sell. More often they only succeed in putting the consumer on edge.

Remember the consumer has control over the content they see. They are able to change sites with the click of a button. Selling to online consumers means not hitting them with product offers and low rates. It means finding out what they are looking for and responding to that need. It means providing them with the information they are looking for and offering them an opportunity to buy.

What this means is selling your customers on a concept, brand, dependability, service, or quality, not on a product. How many times have you entered a store to buy an inexpensive product that satisfies your very basic needs, only to find yourself faced with a brand you don't quite trust or don't want to have your friends see you using? How many times have you walked out of the store with a more expensive product simply because it made you feel better?

Creating an online brand that sells your customer means assessing all the information you have about your customer and your competition and finding where the opportunity exists. Regardless of the product category, there will always be an opportunity to promote such benefits as low price, high value, status, or leading edge technology. However, these benefits are not the key to success. Establishing a brand that side-steps direct competition is; and this means finding a niche that has not been filled.

Product benefits define your product's category. Establishing a brand within the product's category defines your product. If your product competes in a low-priced category, your opportunity is not to underbid your competition. This will only put you into a bidding war. If your competitors tout leading edge technology, trying to outdo them will put you into a race for technology.

Your opportunity lies in your ability to create a brand that supersedes your product's category. Instead of lowering your price to beat your competition, match their price and create better customer service, or exceed their price and promote incredible reliability. Either way, you are creating an image for your product that breaks out of the competitive race. The secret to winning with this strategy is finding out what the consumer wants in your category and delivering on it—but, above all, make sure you can deliver on it.

Accomplishing this does not mean taking a logo and creating a Web site around it. It means creating branded content that supports your positioning to the consumer. This does not simply mean providing answers to frequently asked questions (FAQs), it means providing a quick, personalized response to customer's needs.

On the Internet, advertising moves beyond just promoting consumer benefits. For the first time, every company and product has the opportunity to create a Niketown or a Disney Store. To do this, means going beyond a brochure. It means creating the sites, sounds, and experiences that you want associated with your product. This does not mean spending millions. This does not mean filling a Web site with the latest technologies. It means looking at your customer and creating an online presence they will respond to and they will remember as being different from the competition.

Developing the Brand—The First Step in Building a Relationship

Creating a Personality[6]

Relationships are not built on logos. They are built on personalities. The first step to creating a personality that people respond to requires thinking of the product as a persona rather than as an object.

For some of you, the first response is why. After all, people buy products based on benefits and that product's ability to satisfy specific needs. That is true, but the difference between buying similar products within the same price range lies in the implied benefits associated with brand personality. The ability to stand out in a competitive or crowded category is dependent on a product's personality.

Although the manufacturers may disagree, most people find few differences between a Lexus and a Mercedes that affect their comfort or ability to drive. The differences that exist are reflected in the brand's personality. One targets an older driver who wants comfort, while the other targets a younger driver who "wants to feel the road." The same holds true for established online brands. There are probably few differences in the service provided or in the price of a book ordered from Amazon.com or Barnes & Noble's book.com, but perhaps Amazon appeals to a younger audience intent on breaking away from the bookstores of his or her parents, or perhaps Barnes & Noble implies greater trust.

The point is every product is facing more competition. This means the points of differentiation are becoming fewer and fewer, and the value of the brand becomes increasingly important in the final purchase decision. As you may guess, the personality of the consumer is the guiding force for the personality of the product.

---

[6] An excellent example of developing an effective and consistent online brand can be found in the Bikini.com case study.

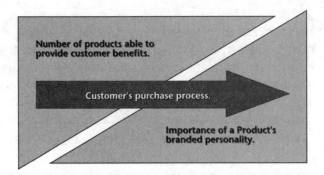

Growing Importance of the Brand in the Purchase Decision

So how do we create a personality for a product? It's easy. First, using the list of product benefits that you created, determine where your product's strengths and weaknesses lie. Ask yourself, is your product of better quality than the competition? Is it less expensive? Does it look better? Is it a better value for the money? Is it a luxury item? These benefits will define its category.

Based on this category, find out who your primary customer will be. Ask yourself, who is your product going to be used by? What kind of person would purchase this product? Do they value style over function? If the product is a computer, will a graphic designer or a business executive be using it and what will their characters be like? Will that person be a small business owner or part of a large corporation? Your goal is to identify your primary customer, not just by age and gender, but by personality; by what is important to them. The personality of your product should reflect the personality of your primary customer.

This does not mean the personality should appeal to all executives aged 25–34 who make more than $80,000. It means the personality should appeal to the creative executive who likes to stay on the leading edge of technology and works for a small edgy design firm that produces Web sites.

Remember that you are creating a product to which your consumer will respond. To do this, everything from its design to its presentation must reflect that person's personality. If you fail to do this, you risk presenting your consumer with a conflicting message—and what is the consumer more likely to buy? A product that he or she is unsure of or a product that reflects who they are?

If you are still unsure of who that person is, look at your competition's ads, pick up appropriate magazines, use anything you can to get a glimpse of your customer. Based on this information, write a page about this person. Include what is important to them and how other advertisers promote to them. Do not write any product benefits into this description. Instead, only write about their personality.

Developing the Personality into an Online Brand

The brand is more than just a logo. It is the look and feel your presence represents. It is more than just the text you use, it is also the way in which it is written. Developing an identifiable brand from a personality requires the creation of a physical image. This means identifying colors and designs to which your customers will respond. Again, you might look at existing advertising or magazines to help create an image your customer will respond to, but this does not mean copying what someone else has done. It means getting as much information as possible and building a unique look and feel for your product.

If your customer is a conservative business executive, perhaps the colors are black, white, and gray with a linear pattern. If your primary customer is a snowboarder, your image may be louder, flashier, and more exciting. Whichever it is, gather as much information on what that customer wants and use it to develop your online presence and your product's package.

At the same time, you will want to begin thinking of a tag line—an identifiable phrase that personifies your product. This is one sentence that describes the essence of the brand to the target audience. It is, in effect, an extremely short summary of your brand's personality page. Again, this has nothing to do with product benefits, because they will change over time. Instead, this line should reflect a factor your customer will associate with and respond to. "Just do it." "Have it your way." "We're Number 2; We try harder." All of these are tag lines that do more than describe a product benefit. They describe exactly what the brand is about.

If your customer works in a fast-paced industry where only the strong survive—then say it. If your customer is a creative thinker where the only limitations should be beyond the clouds—then say it. If your customer is in an industry where value and thrift are all important—then say it—but say it in five words or less.

To create a tag line, take ten key words from your personality page. For each word, write two sentences that reflect the implications of that word, then review each sentence to see which best reflects the product's personality and to which your primary audience will best respond. No matter how sure you are of your tag line, test it. Ask friends, associates, even potential customers for their feedback on this. This tagline will go on every element of your online presence, so make sure it reflects who you are. You may be surprised at their answers.

Leveraging the Brand

Now that you have developed a look and feel for your brand, the worst thing you can do is let it sit there. An essential element to creating a strong brand is providing the consumer with a consistent image.

When people say "Mercedes," they know what the product stands for; when people say "McDonald's," they know exactly what kind of service and product they are going to receive. This is because the personality of each product is reflected in more than just the text and images of the advertising. It is reflected in the sales approach taken, in the service manuals provided, and in the people hired. Maintaining a brand is more than creating consistent advertising, it means creating a personality that is reflected in every aspect of the product. Creating one look, one feel, and one image for the consumer requires more than advertising, it requires an ongoing effort.

At a minimum, you need to start by incorporating a consistent logo and tag line on everything that comes from your company. From business cards and letters, to press releases and advertising, to Web sites and emails, a consistent image should be portrayed. Without this, every company risks confusion in the marketplace as to what exactly is being sold, and with whom they are dealing.

If you look at the Bikini.com Web site, you see fun. If you telephone their offices, you hear the Bikini.com theme song. If you visit their offices, you see surfboards and palm trees, Hawaiian shirts, and hula skirts even though they are in the middle of Manhattan. As everyone says, it's not just a company, it's a lifestyle. That's branding!

Focus, Focus, Focus

The Internet is a double-edged sword. There is so much information out there that anyone can create a Web site on anything and everything. It is a trap far too many people fall into. Too many people begin with a targeted business idea, then, as they start developing their online presence, they expand it, encompassing more and more information. After all, most of the information is free and it makes for a larger Web site. Snap, the trap just closed.

It takes time to collect, manage, and update the information. Once you have an online presence, it is far too easy to let a portion of your site fall behind. Ask any Webmaster if they have all the staff they need and can handle all the day-to-day management of their site. I don't know of one who will answer yes.

Even before launching your site, you will have more than enough work to maintain, market, and promote your site without adding extraneous information. More important, excess content dilutes the focus of a Web site or Web presence. It takes the consumer's eyes away from the real reason they are there—to learn more about your product and to buy. With hundreds of options to choose from, the last thing you need is another distraction.

The best way to avoid this trap is to set a goal of where the business wants to be and when it wants to be there. Too often companies think they will figure it out as they move along. Often those companies find themselves a year further down the road following a direction they never intended to follow, or including bells and whistles that do little to help them reach their goals. They fall into the trap of trying to do everything and accomplishing nothing.

The only way around this is to focus, focus, focus! This means creating a plan and sticking to it. Once your business is up and running, by all means expand, but not until you own your niche. A jack-of-all-trades sells exactly that. Jack.

Setting Goals and Objectives

You have heard it before, and you will hear it again. The Internet is a double-edged sword. It's all out there, free to the touch and just a click away, but your customer doesn't want everything. They only want what interests them. With thousands of sites to choose from, the last thing your customer wants is a confusing mass of information that only provides one-tenth of the information they need.

The only way to prevent this from happening is to create a set of goals and objectives for your online presence. Not only will this help to keep you focused, it will tell you if your efforts are paying off. It will help you determine whether to put more money into the Internet, wait until the Internet matures, or even re-position your efforts to take advantage of a better opportunity.

You know your product better than anyone else. You know what you are trying to achieve. You know when you want to achieve it. You know what your competition is doing. Forget about tomorrow; it's over before you know it. Think three years out. Think realistically but aggressively of where you want to be. Think in terms of site traffic, revenue, audience size, use of newsletters, chats, creation of partnerships with other entities on- and offline. Most importantly, think in terms of your brand. How do you want people to think about it? How big do you want it to be—global, national, regional in scope; what associations do you want involved with it? Write down EVERYTHING you can think of, not just a paragraph, but a page or more. This should go beyond just financial goals, and into how you literally want to feel about your site.

Now, with your three-year goal in mind, begin to work backward. Think where you need to be in one year to achieve your three-year goal. Now, determine where you need to be at the end of six months to achieve that. Now, write down ten tasks that will take you to your six-month goal, and draw a line through the bottom five. Focus your energies on the top five; when those are done, you can approach the next five. Trust me, you will not have the time or energy to do everything that needs to be done, so focus on a few things you can do effectively.

CONCLUSION

At this point you should have a very focused outline of what your business is, who your audience is, what your brand is, and most importantly, what your goals are for taking your business onto the Internet. Without these elements, you may not be guaranteeing failure, but you are guaranteeing a very sizable increase in the cost it will take to succeed at best.

No, the exercises in this section are not the most fun part of creating an online business. However, they are probably the most important. Take the time. Explore your product and your audience. Write down your goals. Do this before moving forward. Only by knowing who you are marketing to can you attempt to sell to them. That is true whether you are selling an actual product, attracting an audience to read your publication, or building a brand.

CHAPTER THREE

Building Online Content to Drive Your Business

The goal of every business is to sell product. Whether that product is an identifiable object or an intangible service, the process is the same. In the offline world, a marketing campaign is created that drives potential customers to the product using identifiable product benefits. Once there, it is up to the sales team to close the sale.[7] The Internet works the same way.

What makes the Internet so different is where the product is advertised and sold. Traditionally, consumers pick up a magazine, watch a television program, or listen to a particular radio station depending on their preferences. Advertisers then place advertising based on that program's ability to deliver their intended audience. The problem is traditional advertising interrupts the consumer's experience. It breaks into radio programs, it cuts into television shows, it separates magazine articles, which is why advertising is facing the problem it has today. It is far less effective than it was 20 years ago because the consumer is aware of what the advertiser is trying to do. They quickly flip the page, go to the kitchen for a snack, or change the radio to more music.

On the Internet, the process is similar, but the consumer has far greater control over what they see and the advertiser has far greater control over how advertising is run. Because of this, to be effective, advertising must be far less intrusive than ever before. Not only must they create advertising that their customer responds to, advertisers must do it in a

---

[7] In a publication, the product is the advertising space they are trying to sell. For the advertiser, the identifiable benefit is the ability to reach a targeted audience based on the quality of the publication's content.

way that does not interrupt the customer's experience. This means incorporating the advertisement into the content—hence content marketing.

In content marketing, content is created to provide consumers with the information they seek. Readers visit the content based on their need for information. Instead of trying to hammer a consumer with a consistent advertising message, the advertiser is attracting the consumer to the message with information they want. Because the reader has opted to visit a web site they have pre-qualified themselves as an interested consumer and potential customer. Based on the quality of the content and its ability to sell, the consumer may respond by making a purchase, or may return at a later time. The real benefit of content marketing is its ability to create a solid relationship with the consumer earlier in the sales cycle.

Online marketing means giving consumers the information they seek, providing them with a resource they can rely on, and being their partner in the purchase decision. Effective online marketing means incorporating the advertiser's message into the content itself in a non-obtrusive manner. When done correctly, this brings the advertiser and the consumer together in a friendly environment. That environment is called branded content.

WHY BRANDED CONTENT DELIVERS A BETTER MESSAGE

Consumers Respond to Content

Although established brands can draw consumers into a given Web site, content is what keeps them coming back. On the Internet, a brand is reflected in the style and depth of the content, not in the logo. Yes, there are implied characteristics that go with a brand's logo, but unless those characteristics come through in the content it is an empty Web site and the consumer will treat it as such. On the Internet a logo graphic is not enough to represent the brand because the Web site is the brand.

In a store, a customer might initially look for an IBM computer or a Maytag washer only to find a better product from a lower-priced competitor. If a customer enters a Web site looking for information about laptop computers and only finds one brand represented, chances are they will continue to look for more information on other Web sites. The answer is not to create a Web site that only represents one product or one brand. Remember the consumer wants information, and will continue looking for information regardless of where it is. The key is to provide the consumer with enough information to satisfy their needs, and at the same time sell them on a given brand or product. How to do this? Create a comparison of competitive products to help the consumer's purchase decision, but be honest and say why yours is the best.

On the Internet consumers are looking for information. They do not have to redial a phone or travel to another store. They merely have to click a mouse. So, while a brand may lead them to a given Web site, it is the quality of the content that keeps them. By creating a guide to help a potential customer become an educated consumer, any brand has the opportunity of creating an ongoing relationship and positioning itself as the brand to trust when it comes time to buy. After all, who would you rather buy from, someone you know and trust, or someone who is trying to sell to you?

Branded Content Is Not Advertising

Other than building an actual store, the Internet is the only medium that can create a truly branded environment. By selecting the audio, video, text, and graphics that goes into online content, a company can control all aspects of the consumer's experience. This is the key to effective on-line marketing—developing branded content. By carefully using online tools, marketers are able to initiate and develop a conversation with their customers that builds relationships.

The first component of any online marketing effort is the creation of branded content. Branded content is simply content that reflects the characteristics of a given brand. It mirrors the look and feel of the product and echoes the personality throughout. As you will see later in this book, effective branded content is consumer-driven content that continues to support and reflect a given brand. Rankit.com is an example of how a leading brand has developed branded content targeting the college student. It provides information every student wants to see, and brands itself at the same time as offering opportunities to buy.

What separates branded content from advertising is that branded content addresses the consumers' needs by providing them with the information or entertainment they are seeking. Similar to the classic advertorial, branded content does not scream a given brand's attributes. It incorporates them into a context to which the consumer responds. In effect, branded content takes the brand off the billboard and puts it into action.

An excellent example of branded content can be found on Life-saver's site—candystand.com. Here, instead of promoting the benefits of its products, it has created games that incorporate each of its products, building the brand's image as fun.

Just as a brand is developed from a product's personality, the effective promotion of a brand on the Internet must include incorporating that personality in all aspects of online content.

CREATING BRANDED CONTENT TO WHICH YOUR CUSTOMERS WILL RESPOND

It should be no surprise at this point that in order for your customers to like your content, it must respond to their needs. Branded content is the first line in a conversation. It is the opener to a longer conversation. If that first line doesn't capture the attention of your customer, they will never respond.

Identify Competitive Weaknesses and Find Partners to Exploit Them

In the last part we completed an exercise to identify your competition by their strengths and weaknesses. Now is the time to use it. You should have a list that bullets the strengths and weaknesses of your competition. You will need to select two pieces of information from this list. The first deals with content, the second with design and programming.

Content

You need to create an online presence that stands out from your competition. Regardless of what they have done, they will have left an opportunity for you. Your goal is to create an online presence that takes advantage of that opportunity. Once you own your niche, you can begin to build out into other niches until you have a very wide and robust presence. Do not try to do it all at once, or you will miss your focus. If your competitors' Web sites focus only on their products, create a product comparison that provides the consumer with a tool. If their site compares every product available, focus on just one customer benefit and build a site with more information than the customer can find anywhere else.

Start to look at content in two ways. The first type of content is known as evergreen. Like the tree, this is product information that does not change from month to month and that consumers can expect to find at almost any site. It will be the most basic information that you need in order to compete. It will most likely be on every other site, but consumers will want it because it provides the background information they will refer to.

On a financial services site, this may be a description of the various types of stocks, bonds, and securities being traded, or it may be a history of the stock market, or a background on economics. These are tools people may want to refer to, even though they are not the most up-to-date stock quotes.

The second type of information is updated frequently and is what will set you apart. What type of content this includes is found in the weaknesses of your competition's sites. From your previous list take the top five weaknesses and pick the one or two you perceive as most important or the ones you can best address. This information will be the content that sets your site apart from the competition and will be the key benefit of your online presence. For the most part, this will be the up-to-date information that consumers are seeking. It is the information that will change on a daily, weekly, or monthly basis. In our previous example, this information would be the stock quotes.

The question of whether a site should be primarily fresh or evergreen depends on the site itself. According to a 1999 Forrester Research study, 75 percent of online consumers return to their favorite sites for the strong content and 54 percent return for regular turnover of information. Most believe if 70 percent to 90 percent of a site is evergreen content it will be more than enough to maintain ongoing interest.

If other sites fail to provide breaking news, supply it. If other sites fail to provide customer bulletin boards, find a way to manage them. If other sites do not have resume boards, create them. As you will find, the content that consumers need on a day-to-day basis will be the content they bookmark and return to, and this is how you begin to create a relationship with your consumers and turn them into customers. Just make sure you will be able to maintain the fresh content. If you have to err, err on the side of evergreen content. You can always increase the level of fresh content according to the demands of your customer.

Design

There will always be an opportunity to create an identifiable statement with your design. Remember the branding exercise? Take everything you learned about your customer and have that direct your design.

Everything about your site should reflect the needs and expectations of your consumer. From the use of colors to the type font, everything should reflect your ideal customer.[8]

After you have looked at your customer, take a look at your competition. Look at the elements they have incorporated into their sites. Decide which are important and which are not. Based on your resources, decide on which are easy to manage and which are difficult. Remember quality over quantity.

If your competition has taken form over function their Web sites are probably slow to download. Build a fast site that gives the consumer what they want without waiting. If your competition has a text site without much interaction, enable the consumer to take part in the site and enable them to interact with their peers. There will always be opportunities to take advantage of a creative niche that your competition hasn't approached. If you have trouble finding one, this is a very good sign that you need an outside design firm to help you.

Quality over Quantity

". . . What, and leave showbiz?" For those of you too young to remember, it's the punch line of a very old joke. Suffice it to say, remember you are in the business of selling. You are selling a product, not creating the next Laurence of Arabia. Yes, the Internet is about content, but if that content fails to build your business, then you are in the wrong business.

The Internet is a delivery system. It is similar to television or radio. For the most part, television viewers do not care what company produces a program or what network a program is on. They only care about its content—how good is the action, how well is it acted, or how compelling is the script. I have yet to hear someone say they prefer CBS to NBC or ABC. I have heard a great many people still rave about The Honeymooners, I Love Lucy, Cheers, or Seinfeld even after the programs have gone into reruns.

Like television, a Web site is a vehicle for its content. Consumers are more concerned with the quality of the content than the URL it resides on, and loyalty is a very fleeting commodity. People will remain loyal to your Web site and your brand as long as it continues to provide them with the content they are seeking.

---

[8] The Bikini.com case study is an excellent example of how to create a presence that reflects a given brand.

As your online business grows, you will be very tempted to increase your content. Be very careful that growth does not interfere with the quality of your business.

WHERE TO BUILD BRANDED CONTENT

One of the biggest mistakes far too many people make is in thinking that a Web site is the only way to create an online presence or do business on the Internet. The Internet is comprised of a number of electronic systems. These include such components as the World Wide Web, email, BBS, and independent online services such as America Online, each of which is described here in detail. Creating a successful online business goes back to determining the goals and objectives and identifying the best component to use.

Some products may not be best suited to a Web site. Some audiences are better reached through email. Some goals may be better served by developing a micro-site that lives within a larger Web site. Some brands may not be well served by the World Wide Web's audience at all. The key is to look at your audience and overall objectives before deciding on the best ways to reach both of them.

Remember, like television, the Internet is a delivery system for your product's message. It is a way to connect your product with your customer. The secret is finding the best way to achieve this.

As we have seen, the benefits found in television advertising are very different than print, radio, or outdoor. Just as traditional advertising incorporates a number of different mediums to create an advertising campaign, an online campaign is best created from a number of different online elements. It is up to you to decide which elements will best help you reach your audience.

For a product like Tylenol, a Web site is probably not the best use of its money. Just consider how many people would visit Tylenol.com. Not many, especially considering how most of us would rather not think of pain relief until we are in pain, and at that point, looking on the Internet for relief is probably not the way many of us would approach the problem. We would go out and buy Tylenol, Excedrin, or any other product that was handy.

Instead, if Tylenol created a series of micro-sites that nested on other Web sites, they could reach a much larger audience with a more pertinent message. One micro-site that listed ways to relieve stress for the small business owner could be placed on several small business Web sites.

Another on how to prevent sports injuries could be placed on sports-related Web sites. Another on reducing the discomfort of pregnancy could be placed on maternal health sites. Yet another on the pharmaceutical advantages of various painkillers could be placed on a site targeting medical practitioners.

Without having to manage an entire Web site or spend money to promote it, Tylenol could reach the consumers most likely to use its products without having to spend the money creating, managing, and promoting a Web site of its own. More importantly, rather than creating a blatant advertisement that most of us are likely to dismiss as pure promotion, Tylenol is providing the consumer with information they can use, and will likely return to when they need it again.

Taking this one step further, if Tylenol were to incorporate a cents-off coupon the consumer could download, it could track the success of its online efforts directly. In this way, Tylenol could create a brand-driven marketing campaign that produced bottom-line results easily, quickly, and efficiently.

As with the Tylenol example, the goal of taking a business online is not to create a Web site. It is to find the best way to position a product and deliver its message to its audience in an environment where the consumer will respond positively.

For other companies, the cost of building and maintaining a Web site may not justify the benefits. The idea of creating a new Web site to introduce a product is a risky venture. It takes time and money to promote it and drive consumers to its pages. For some products, it may be wiser to leverage the traffic of a larger site by building a content area that it can maintain without the technical problems of maintaining a server. In short, a Web site may not be the most efficient way to reach the right audience.

For other products, the Internet may not be able to deliver the right audience at this time. Chanel is a world class brand. It has prestige, clout, and a following that includes some of the wealthiest consumers in the world. It also has a Web site, but who does this site reach? Take a look at the demographics of the Internet and they are surely not the audience buying Chanel.

Although Chanel has done a very good job creating its online presence, consider if the Web audience accurately represents its brand. If you think it does, take a look at *www.gap.com* and see which one represents an Internet brand.

The fact is, Chanel's customers know who Chanel is. To promote it to the general Web audience risks damaging a very well positioned brand that only appeals to a very select consumer. Instead, Chanel could use the Internet to provide real benefits to its clientele. The cost of maintaining a Web site that promotes the Chanel brand to the general online audience could probably be better spent maintaining a monthly email to its existing clientele with fashion news and information to cement its relationship, or in creating an online members-only club to benefit its preferred customers, or perhaps creating a co-branded area within the *Cosmopolitan* Web site to leverage their name and cachet.

As you can see, depending on the objectives of a company, developing a Web site may not be the best way to use the Internet at this time. Yes, the Internet will change. Yes, it will morph into something else as technology advances. When that happens, advertisers will need to review and revise their plans. However, until then, the Internet should be used for the medium that it is.

As we have said, the use of various online elements to build your business should be directly related to the goals and objectives you are trying to achieve.

Email/Newsletters

Today, email is one of the most widely given reasons for being on the Internet. Originally a system created to send text from one computer to another, email now serves millions of people worldwide allowing them to attach files that go beyond text and simple charts to include images, audio, and video files.

Today there are numerous email newsletters that include everything from up-to-the-minute stock alerts to news, recipes, and even jokes. Some of these are maintained on a subscription basis. Others are supported by paid advertising. Still others have been created to augment a Web site. Regardless, email based newsletters are an excellent way to maintain a relationship with the consumer by delivering timely information.

Suffice it to say, with all the horror stories about what happens to spammers, any email program should always be opt-in, that is, where people request to be included on the list. If you decide to send unsolicited email, I leave the consequences to you.

Benefits

- Cost—The cost of maintaining a moderately sized (up to 5,000 or 10,000 names) email list is very little. Aside from some initial programming, it does not require a large server or much technical skill to maintain a list. An email list can easily be maintained for the cost of a basic Web site hosting.

- Creating a conversation—The strongest benefit for email is its ability to create an ongoing conversation with the customer. Unlike traditional advertising, email allows the consumer to respond instantly to the information sent. Not only does this allow them to voice their opinions or concerns, it allows businesses to ask the consumer how they feel about a new product, a new service or a redesign of a Web site. Email not only provides invaluable information, it brings the consumer into the communication process and builds an ongoing conversation.

- Research and testing—This is not a novel idea, but finding out what a consumer thinks about a new product or design before it goes into production does more than create a product consumers want. It saves time and money. What do you have to do to accomplish this? Simply ask the consumer in an email. Best of all, they don't have to respond immediately. They can do so when they have time to sit and think.

- Expanding the Web site—Instead of attracting a consumer to the Web site, why not send a portion of the Web site to your consumer? Remember vertical content? Individual consumers rarely want all of a Web site's content. They are more interested in a specific aspect of it. Why not create a series of emails that offer content on various subjects? New content can be promoted with a newsletter directing visitors back to the site.

- Building relationships—If you own a Web development firm, why not create a series of emails that target the business owner interested in creating a Web-based business? Each email could provide useful information on the design, development, and maintenance of a Web site. Offer this as a service from your Web site as a resource for the small business owner searching for information. When it comes time to choose a firm, who are they more likely to rely on? A design firm they have heard from every week, who has helped them arrive at a decision on how to proceed, or a firm they barely know?

Drawbacks

- Content creation—As with everything on the Internet, success means time. It takes time to create content that the consumer really wants. Success of an email campaign is found in the value of the information provided. If the email is to provide news and information it has to be timely or people will ask to be removed. If the email provides jokes, they must not only be funny, they must be consistent. Everyone has a different sense of humor. Trust me from experience, you cannot serve everyone's sensibilities.

• Time—Creating fresh content and managing a list takes time. If you try an email list, start off on a weekly or monthly basis. Assess how much time it will take to create the content before doing anything more aggressive, and assess how much interest your recipients will have in the information before they tire of receiving it.

Process

The first step in developing an email newsletter is creating content. If you are sending out a monthly email, make sure you have six months of content. If you are sending out a weekly email, make sure you have eight weeks of content. If you are sending out a daily email, make sure you have four weeks of content. You will fall behind at one point or another, so make sure you are covered.

Hire a programmer to develop or adapt an email delivery program that will meet your needs. This can range from a simple program that allows you to manually insert information into the email format via an FTP connection or a complete admin server that allows you to update lists, email, contents, and other components of the process automatically.[9]

That is all it takes. Yes, it sounds simple, but if it is so simple, why aren't more people doing it? It is more difficult than you think to develop and maintain content that people want to receive.

Micro-site

For any number of reasons some products may not be well suited to attracting an audience to a Web site. A product may not be compelling enough, the cost of creating and maintaining a Web site may be prohibitive, the cost of driving traffic to a Web site may not justify the expense. Whatever the reason, some businesses should consider creating micro-sites that live on other Web sites rather than creating a single Web site.

Other businesses can use a micro-site to promote a large Web presence. As you will see, promoting a Web site by creating a "teaser site" that

---

[9] Your familiarity with the uses of FTP and Telnet should dictate which way you go.

draws the reader back to the larger site is one of the most effective ways to advertise on the Internet. Similarly, preempting a Web site with a smaller presence can be used to develop an audience before the final Web site is even launched.

A micro-site is nothing more than a small Web site that lives on a larger Web site. In our Tylenol example, this might mean creating a series of informational micro-sites that provide specific content to everything from small business owners to sports enthusiasts.

The key, once again, lies in creating specific content that targets the needs of a specific consumer.

Benefits

- Cost—Because a micro-site is smaller than a full Web site, it is less expensive to create and maintain. That is not to say a micro-site should not have all the interactivity and components of a full Web site, it merely does not have to be as large.
- Traffic/Advertising—The biggest advantage of a micro-site is the fact that it is nested on a larger, more popular Web site. Not only does this take advantage of that site's traffic, it requires less advertising to promote it. The fact that a micro-site can quickly draw large traffic numbers without the cost of advertising is a tremendous benefit not only in money but in time.
- Branding—Depending on where a Web site is nested, a new product or unknown brand can leverage the value of the hosting site. Such elements as quality, value, and integrity that many consumers associate with a given brand are implied with the micro-site/host-site relationship. For an unknown brand, this can be extremely beneficial in positioning itself in the market.

Drawbacks

- Loss of control—Most micro-sites will be to some degree at the mercy of the hosting site, not only in their programming requirements, but also in their design elements. Consider this strongly when entering into an agreement with another Web site. Although in my experience most of these issues can be negotiated into a win-win relationship, be very aware of what you want before you enter into any agreement.
- Multiple site maintenance—Although a micro-site is smaller and will require less resources to develop it, the cost of maintaining

fresh content on several micro-sites can take its toll. As with any online presence, make sure you have the time to create fresh, interesting content that meets the consumer's needs.

Process

The concept behind a micro-site is that you provide valuable content to the hosting site, content that the consumer wants to see that adds editorial value to the hosting site. This is content that will help them increase their page views, content that is free. In return, you will receive a well-branded site with higher levels of traffic than if you had created your own Web site.

The development of a micro-site is identical to the development of a Web site. Since a micro-site relies on another Web site for its URL, some elements of design and programming may depend on the host site. However a win-win situation can usually be negotiated.

To do this, one must first find several Web sites that have suitable content and traffic levels. Suitable means having content that compliments your product or your brand and that is within the same or similar category as your product. It also means having content that will not compete with your product, not only for today, but for the next year and beyond.

It then means contacting that Web site's marketing director or Webmaster and proposing an agreement whereby you are providing them with content for use on their site. Fine points of this can include revenue share of any advertising sold on the micro-site, how often and in what ways the micro-site can be updated, what the technical limitations and requirements for the micro-site are, who owns the content, and other issues.

To introduce a micro-site to a possible host, I have found it easiest to create a one-page overview for the proposed micro-site before contacting any potential hosting sites. Not only will this help to outline what you want to achieve, it will provide the hosting site with an easy-to-understand outline that will move the entire process quickly.[10]

Sponsoring Content

Sponsoring content can be as simple as paying a Web publisher to have a logo placed on existing content. It can be as involved as developing new content that is hosted on an existing Web site. For many advertisers

---

[10] See appendix 6 for a sample one-sheet overview.

this makes more sense and provides a better return than developing and maintaining a new Web site of their own.

Creating an online presence requires more than just designing and building a Web site. It means promoting that Web site, updating the content, and responding to the needs of the readers. As almost every online marketer has discovered, creating a Web presence is an ongoing project that requires a lot of time and energy. At the same time, some marketers find their products or services will never attract a very large audience. For those advertisers who either do not want the upkeep of a Web presence, or whose products will not attract a large audience, the concept of sponsoring existing content or hosting content on another site should be considered.

In our previous example of a pain reliever, it would be far more profitable for the makers of Tylenol to create content that could be sent to a variety of sites than to create their own Web site. After all, how many people would truly visit Tylenol.com every day? People simply do not want to think about a headache until they have one. However, creating a series of tips on stress reduction that would be hosted on a number of small business sites would deliver their message to millions without the cost or time involved in maintaining and marketing their own Web site.

Benefits

- Content creation—For the most part, the benefits of sponsored content are similar to those of a micro-site. However, since sponsored content is incorporated into an existing Web site's content, it requires even less work to design and implement.

- Maintenance costs—Sponsored content is maintained by the host site which means the sponsor is even further removed from the publishing process and its costs. Each of these factors is determined by the terms of the sponsorship deal, but for many products and services, sponsored content can be an inexpensive and profitable way to gain an online presence without having to maintain it on a daily basis.

Drawbacks

- Loss of control—As with a micro-site, the sponsor is to some degree at the mercy of the hosting site. Unlike a micro-site, a sponsor has even less control over the programming requirements and design elements. Again, most of these issues can be negotiated into a win-win relationship, so be very aware of what you want before you enter into any agreement.

Process

The first step is to identify a Web publisher whose content supports your product or category. This does not mean finding a Web publisher who is willing to sell the editorial integrity of their content to an advertiser. Online readers are very suspicious of content. If it looks as if that content is just promotional material, they will move on quickly. It means finding a publisher whose content will attract your audience.

The best sites for sponsored content will be able to provide substantial traffic, deliver your targeted audience, and have an established brand name which will help to establish your product. For some products this may mean an online newspaper. For others it may mean an entertainment Web site. Regardless, assess the needs of your product and brand to determine what type of content would be most appropriate, then assess the publisher to ensure they will maintain the quality of your content.

Web Site

For the right brand, a Web site is one of the best ways to promote and sell its products. It provides the most control over the development and maintenance of branded content. It also provides the greatest opportunity to create content that the consumer will respond to.

The ability to create the look and feel of a customer's experience, to track a customer's visit, to generate and close sales, and to perform research makes it one of the best mediums to build a brand and manage online commerce. These are some of the most important reasons for creating and maintaining a Web site. However, regardless of whether your goal is to sell products, develop a publication, or promote a brand, if you do not need to have complete control over the content and sales process one of the other models may be a more effective way to market your product.

To use all the benefits a Web site can provide means creating a brand-driven campaign that makes the product come alive to the consumer. How does today's marketer do this? By creating content that responds to the consumer's needs.

Remember content is what drives consumers to a given Web site. Content is also what holds the advertiser's message. Content enables the advertiser to develop a relationship with the consumer that meets both the needs of the advertiser and the consumer. So not only should it promote the brand, but also it should act like a salesperson and drive the consumer into a comfortable position to buy. Look at Barnes & Noble. Every page points to a checkout counter.

Benefits

A well-designed and properly implemented Web site is the cornerstone of almost any online marketing effort. The ability to capture information and create customer interaction on a Web site is what creates the richest conversation between the product and its customer. More than any other tool, a Web site provides consumers with the information they are seeking and enables a company to truly brand its product or service.

A Web site by itself is almost useless. However, when combined with rich content and an integrated advertising program, the Web site becomes the cornerstone of an effective marketing effort. This means being able to create a campaign that can brand a product, develop consumer relationships, and create a sales channel.

The most valuable benefits to creating a Web site over other online content is control over the development and management of content and the consumer's interaction.

- Interaction—For marketers and advertisers, a Web site allows direct interaction with consumers. No other medium allows instantaneous two-way communication. Whether it is as simple as providing a direct response mechanism for consumers or collecting data for an auto-responder, the Internet allows marketers to talk to and address the concerns of consumers, turning consumers into customers, and customers into brand loyal users.

- Branding—A well-designed Web site allows marketers to truly brand their product. Every aspect of the environment is created and managed, much like the way in which Disney controls the look and feel of their retail stores. With this in mind a personalized customer experience can be created combining specific graphics, text, sounds, and even video. With the Web as a tool, a savvy marketer can create a truly branded environment with which to approach and convert customers.

- Sales leads—A monitored Web site provides an incredible amount of information on who the consumer is and what they are looking for. Today's marketers are doing more than just promoting and selling products on the Web. They are learning who their customer is, what their habits are, and what they want. From this, they are generating qualified sales leads and closing transactions. Today, companies can take customers from shopping to purchasing without ever having to open a door. If there is any doubt as to the profits that can be made, take a look at some of the case studies in this book.

- Sales team—In today's global and highly competitive market, a sales team needs a tactical advantage over their competition. A Web site can provide just that. Sales presentations and information can be placed on a protected Web site for access anywhere in the world, 24 hours a day. Any sales team can be better equipped to provide sales sheets, product information, even live demonstrations as clients request them on the spot. That gives them an advantage in closing a sale.

- Customer service—Imagine a customer contacting a company at any time of the day throughout the week. With a Web site, customers could have questions answered, receive detailed product information, even bring issues to your attention without ever having to take valuable time from a staff member. A fully interactive customer service area, complete with answers to common questions, not only responds to customer problems and requests, it can gather information without ever making a customer feel put out.

Drawbacks

- Cost—One of the greatest drawbacks to developing and maintaining a Web site is the cost, both in time and money. Depending on the design and content, development of a Web site can cost anywhere from hundreds to hundred of thousands of dollars. However, to effectively promote and maintain a Web site it will cost anywhere from several thousand dollars or more a year for basic site maintenance, to several million for a staff and a marketing program. Be prepared for this. What you gain in control, you pay for in dollars and time.

- Publisher—I do not know of one advertiser who does not call themselves an online publisher. Regardless of their initial efforts, at some point, they cross the line and began developing content. If they don't, their sites either languish or turn into a corporate brochure. The need to respond to their customers' needs turns them into publishers, and that takes time and energy.

FACTORS IN DEVELOPING ONLINE CONTENT

Although this section deals specifically with the development of a Web site, the rules and lessons apply to sponsored content, micro-sites, and even the development of email campaigns. Regardless of what you are creating, remember to always view the content from the consumer's perspective. If the content does not respond to the needs of its readers, they will not read it and they will not return.

Design and Graphics

One Look, One Feel, One Brand

Consumers have hundreds of Web sites to choose from. Each of these competes with yours in one way or another. To make matters worse, consumers are bombarded by hundreds of messages from radio, television, print, and outdoor advertising every day. In a market like this, the only way to differentiate yourself from your competition is to create a consistent image and maintain that image throughout your entire online presence.

Take a look at any successful product on the market and you will see a consistency in its advertising, packaging, and corporate image. That is what you have to create on your Web site—a consistent look and feel regardless of where your consumer is. Just because it is a new medium does not mean the old rules don't apply.

When you design your Web site, create design elements that can be maintained throughout your site. This includes a color scheme, font style, corporate logos, or even navigation buttons. Anyone should be able to enter your site at any page and instantly know what the site is for and who you are. As you will see later, few people actually enter a site through the front door. Some come in from the side, some from the back, and some clamber in through the window. Be prepared for them and create a consistent image the consumer can remember—that means creating one look, one feel, and one brand.

Consistent Design, Not Boring Design

Consistency between pages is the key to having your customer remember who you are. Taken too far, it can become the road to a boring site. One look does not mean repeating the same color and icon over and over again. It means establishing a color and design palate that reflects the brand, but there is no reason that palate cannot be augmented to help bring individual sections to life.

If the central color is yellow, one section can be augmented with green and another can be augmented with blue. Expanding the central design elements can help identify what each of these sections is about and build on the visitor's experience. Just make sure the green and blue are from the same palette and there is a connection between the designs. It's when each of these elements is put together without a defining feature that the consumer becomes confused.

It's Your House—Own it

Owning your Web site means more than paying the InterNIC fee. It means doing more than identifying every page on your site with a logo. It means supporting your brand with the text and graphics. If you have to use content from another site, rewrite it. Put a spin on it that is uniquely yours, or incorporate some of the elements from your site's design to ensure your customer identifies your brand within it.

With everything you do on the Internet, you have the opportunity to create an online Niketown. The only way to do this is to ensure every element on your domain says one word—YOU!

Tech vs. Traffic

This will be an ongoing question for which there is no right answer. The higher the level of technology within your site, the longer it will take to download, the more plug-ins will be required, and the more problematic your visitor's experience will be. All of this means one thing: Fewer people will be able to reach your content.

Whether to add higher technologies means asking one question— are you willing to give up a larger audience for a showcase, or are you trying to reach as many people as possible? If you are creating a showcase to demonstrate your capabilities as a design firm and your audience is other designers, then going high-tech works. If you are trying to sell books to the general public, then going high-tech will limit the number of people who can access your site.

As with everything else, the decision to go bleeding edge or lowest common denominator depends on your industry. Look at your competition. See what they are doing. Consider your consumer and where they will access your site from (home equals low tech, office equals high bandwidth).

As technology changes, the accessibility to higher technology becomes easier and less expensive. Your capabilities and those of your customer will change. Remain flexible and be ready to adapt new technology as it arrives, but unless you absolutely must, refrain from being the first to use new technology. It has a nasty habit of backfiring at the most inopportune time. Also, if you insist on creating a leading-edge site, consider creating a low-bandwidth version for those who don't want all the bells and whistles. You might be surprised to learn that very few top-level executives have the time to keep up with all the downloads a high-tech site requires.

Navigation and Content Hierarchies

All Roads Lead to Information

In one sense, a Web site serves two purposes. The first is to provide content to its customers. The second is to act as a filter to speed the customer directly to the content they want. Yes, information is what the Internet is all about, but unless the reader can get to it quickly and easily, they'll never make it.

Think in terms of your customer when building a content hierarchy. Ask yourself what information they want and how they will look for it. Create a pyramid with your home page on the top. Then create a level beneath it that divides your content into distinct areas of information based on what the consumer will be looking for. Use the first two levels as directional, to help your customer find exactly what they need. By the third level, the consumer must be able to find the information they are looking for. Avoid going past three levels without giving them what they want.

If you are selling a product, the first level should break your online catalog into sections (e.g., pants, shirts, jackets). The second level should

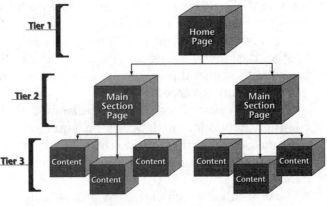

Navigational Hierarchy

divide each section into products (e.g., t-shirts, dress shirts). The third level should enable the customer to buy. If you are providing news, the first level should break the news into content areas, the second level should provide story areas, and the third level should provide the story. Any more levels than this and your customer will be someone else's.

Just as important, your customer must be provided with information as they travel to their destination. An excellent example of this can be found on the *Los Angeles Times'* Web site (*www.latimes.com*). You will find the first two levels guide the reader to the appropriate story, yet they still provide information in the way of story summaries and associated stories that may be of interest to the reader. Not only does this provide users with the opportunity to read other stories, it provides them with an idea of what else is on the site.

Most important, regardless of where they are in your hierarchy, make sure your customer will not have to wait through a long download time to access the data they want. If you have a chart, graph, or video clip a reader might be interested in, create a thumbnail image and let the reader decide if they want to see the entire image. To force a long download time is to ensure the loss of a customer.

The Importance of Vertical Content

For the Consumer

As soon as someone goes online, they began to look for specific information. Even if a person is surfing, they quickly begin to look for a particular subject. A sports fanatic, for instance, does not bookmark the front page of a Web site (e.g., *www.latimes.com*). They bookmark the sports section page (e.g., www.latimes.com/sports), or even better, the page with the baseball stats. If an investor wants to see how her stocks are doing she doesn't bookmark the front page, she bookmarks the page that has her stock quotes. Going right to the information that most affects them simply speeds their journey.

Whether a consumer is looking for a news article or for specific product information, a Web site should reflect this by arranging its information in vertical segments according to the content. Not only does this enable the Web site to attract users according to their needs, it makes it easier for users to navigate to the information they want quickly and easily. To do this effectively, marketers must:

- Identify specific consumer needs and address those needs with specific content categories

- Increase ease of use by arranging content according to its subject matter
- Ensure smooth site navigation by cross-linking relevant content without complicating the consumer's process with too many choices

Examples of this can be found in the way Barnes & Noble separates its content according to author, subject, or publisher, or the way the *Los Angeles Times* separates its content by subject matter. The most important factor is to separate content according to the consumer's needs, not those of the site. After all, they are the ones using the site.

For the Site

Vertical content is easier to promote for the same reasons that it is easier for the consumer to find; it targets the information they need. Because the content is arranged in vertical packages, marketers can identify and target specific consumer needs according to those packages. Remember, when a consumer enters a section of a Web site, it is just like entering a specific store. He or she instantly identifies himself or herself as a potential customer who is interested in a specific category. It's the same reason why supermarkets put all the meats in one aisle, and all personal care items in another. Shoppers are more likely to buy related products.

Additionally, the more specific an area is, the better a marketer can tailor the message to meet the consumer's concerns and needs. With a greater ability to target advertising to a specific online audience, a Web site is better off creating several advertising messages. Ideally, each message follows the brand but addresses specific user needs according to the content of a specific online section. As you will find out later, to promote an entire site may not be the best way to promote a Web presence. It is often better to promote distinct sections according to the specific market segments they appeal to.

Finally, by creating specific sections that target identifiable consumer needs, today's online publisher has a better opportunity to attract advertisers. Advertisers look for a way to reach their target audience for one reason: They are more likely to buy a given product than the general audience is. The ability to deliver an audience that has expressed an interest in sports gives the publisher an advantage in selling ads to a sports store. The same is true for almost any category. However, the only way to achieve this is by creating vertical content packages that target specific consumer interests.

Include Actionable Benefits

Actionable benefits are product benefits the consumer responds to quickly. They may prompt a customer to purchase from an ecommerce site, or entice a reader to view another story on a news site. A 10 percent discount for purchasing now may induce a consumer to buy immediately. A seasonal news section that will only be up for a month entices readers to read now.

Immediacy is one element the Internet lacks. It costs little to keep content on the Web once it has been created, and there is little reason for consumers to hurry back to most sites. After all, where is the information going to go? To create a sense of urgency means telling the consumer this offer or this story is not going to be available for long.

Throughout the sales cycle almost every Web site has an opportunity to induce a purchase decision. The key is to identify where the consumer is in the purchase cycle on each page and place the right inducement on the right page. If someone is looking at general information, they are probably still at the exploratory stage. If someone is looking at prices, they are closer to making an actual purchase. By tailoring an immediate offer around each of these, a Web site can urge consumers into a purchase decision quicker.

Examples of this would include:

1. Information Gathering
   - Offering product samples to elicit trial use
   - Creating informational packages in order to develop a marketable database
2. Pre-sale
   - Providing online coupons or discounts to induce a purchase
   - Providing an upgrade offer for an immediate purchase
3. Sale
   - Providing a money-back guarantee to ensure satisfaction
   - Establishing an open return policy
4. Post Sale
   - Developing online customer service (e.g., FAQ, shipment tracking) to ensure customer satisfaction
   - Creating newsletters for product news and sales for peripheral products
   - Creating bulletin boards to ensure product satisfaction and build customer community

Nav Bars

Too many people enter a Web site and then get lost after three clicks. When this happens, their next move is to type in the words "Yahoo.com" to search for another Web site. Avoid losing your customers by limiting their frustration. Create simple navigation that gives control over your site to the customer. Keep it simple. Keep it fast.

The one element of your site that should never change is your primary navigation bar. It should be a constant that is easy to find and that your customer doesn't have to look for from page to page. The majority of Web designers place this bar on the upper-left side of every Web page or on the top of every Web page. The only answer to creating something tricky and novel is don't. Save tricky for the design if you must, not the navigation.

All primary section pages should be accessible from any page in the site. If there are a large number of subsections within each section, create a secondary navigation bar that appears only when the consumer is in that section.

The primary and secondary navigation bars should be labeled clearly to show your visitors where they are and what else is available. This can be done by highlighting the current section, using a Java script to make it pop, or by any other method you wish. Also, make sure there is a "home" button on every page to allow people to quickly and easily reestablish their location with one simple button.

Limited Choices

Have you ever wondered why car stereos have only eight buttons for preset channels? Or why most of us only place eight phone numbers into memory before forgetting who went where? People are marvels at taking in information. However, we have a limited amount of truly useful information that we refer to on a daily basis.

Do not put twenty links on your home page or it becomes confusing. If you cannot limit your site to eight distinct areas, consider creating two sites. You do not want to overload your customer with too many choices, or they will go to someone who can guide them better.

Site Maps

A site map is often a useful idea. This can be as simple as listing all the pages in outline form. It can be as complex as an interactive page that shows all the links from one page to the next. The answer here is, again, keep it simple. Remember, if someone visits this page they are lost. They do not need to get even more lost.

Developing Content That Works

Words and Pictures

Customers visit your Web site for two reasons: to get information or to be entertained. They do not want a lot of extraneous data that delays their progress. If at any time a customer thinks you are wasting their time, they will leave. Too many pages with unimportant information lead customers to type the words "Yahoo.com," and that is a lost opportunity.

Use language that is direct but reflects your brand. Use bullets to get a series of points across. Divide paragraphs into smaller units. Avoid flowery language unless it is absolutely necessary. Look at your competitors' Web sites. Read their copy. Think how much time it took for them to get an idea across and then do it in less. If you can, you win.

Although some designers disagree, many icons are useless on a Web site. Icons like the STOP sign works because everyone recognizes and responds to it. Icons that people have to learn the meaning of are close to useless in a medium that moves as quickly as the Internet. Be careful when creating a new icon, or when using an unknown icon. For many customers they are merely confusing and for many designers they are merely an excuse to get creative. Remember simple and fast.

Pictures are worth a thousand words, but, like icons, if they do not add to the consumer's experience, don't use them. If a graphic takes 10 seconds to download, it had better be worth it. Graphics that help describe a product or speed the consumer on their way are good. Just make sure your reader thinks so. Provide thumbnails for larger graphics and provide download size and time. This allows the customer who is interested to view the graphic. Those who aren't can continue without a delay.

In the same vein, make sure all images on your site are reduced to the smallest size possible while still being legible. This decreases download times and increases reader time.

Remember, speed of information is critical to success on the Net.

Add Value, Add Value, Add Value

Nobody wants to give it away for free, but if you don't your competition will. The information is out there and your customers will find it. Your only question is, do you want them to find it on your site or on your competition's? Few people will visit a site that doesn't promise a wealth of information. Even fewer will return to a site that fails to deliver what they promised.

The formula is simple—give the consumer the information they want and they will return. Provide them with more information in the form of white papers, additional links, resources, even entertainment and they will continue to return. Give them promotional hype and they will go to a trustworthy source.

Branded content is not hype. Branded content is useful information that incorporates a brand's image. Adding links and additional information to this content adds value and that makes customers happy. Remember, if you don't give it to them, someone else will, and they will have a better chance to win your customer.

How to Create the Content You Need

Fresh vs. Evergreen

The question everyone asks is how to create the content. There are two ways to do this. The first way is to create it yourself. In many ways this process is similar to writing a book report. You gather the information you need and write your text according to what your customers are trying to find. Then you arrange that text into a hierarchy that delivers your information to the consumer quickly and easily. The second way is to identify partners who can supply content to you. As you will see, creating your own content is not always the best way to go.

Before we address how to develop content, we need to know what type of content to develop. There are two types of content: *fresh* and *evergreen*. As its name implies, fresh content is timely and changes often. Fresh content includes daily news stories, stock quotes, weather forecasts, or the ability to track packages. This is usually the most expensive content to maintain and often requires a dedicated person to maintain it.

The second type of content is evergreen. Like the tree, this is content that does not change often. However, it still provides the consumer with useful information. Evergreen content includes historical information, technical data, a loan or mortgage calculator, even beauty tips. It helps to build a rich site and although consumers will not flock to this content, they will want to refer to it often.

Most Web sites provide anywhere from 20 percent to 60 percent in fresh content. The remainder is evergreen. Which type of content is used depends on your industry, your competition, and your customers. If you are not sure how much to create, go back to your research. Find out how much your competitors are using. Look on their bulletin boards and find out if their customers are looking for more or less content, then deliver it.

As you travel through the Internet, you will notice a lot of sites deliver the same content. Almost every newspaper has stock quotes and sport scores. Although not every reader checks this information every day, they want to know this information is available if they need it. If it wasn't, readers would ask themselves, "What are we missing?"

The same holds true for the Internet. Not all the information on a site needs to be original, but it does need to provide the consumer with a rich experience. A lot of content will be the same from site to site and will not change over time. The key to a successful site does not necessarily mean creating new content every day, but it does mean providing information that establishes that site as the one resource for its consumer.

Don't spend your time building every inch of your site. Acquire evergreen content from partners and spend your time creating the content that will truly separate you from your competition and will respond to your consumer's needs.[11]

Content Sharing

After you have determined what kind of content you will need, you will need to determine where to acquire it. If you are going to create it yourself, you know better than any book the type of information you will want to include. If not, I strongly encourage hiring a consultant to determine what will work.

If you are going to acquire it, the best place to start is with your competition. Find out where they acquired their evergreen content and approach those sources. Remember, evergreen content doesn't change, so focus your efforts on finding the most reliable and reputable source or well-known brand you can. These elements will do more for establishing your site as a reference than any advertising you can create. If possible, try to strike a deal that allows you to reformat this information to match the look and feel of your site. It will help brand your site and your image.

However you decide to proceed, the best place to start is by identifying partners who can supply the content you need. After you have done this, assess which ones will provide you with the best brand image, and which will allow you to change the copy and design so that it better

---

[11] A number of businesses have begun to provide syndicated content such as Timeslink and iSyndicate. Resources for each are provided in appendix 2.

reflects your site and your brand. Most content providers will allow this to some degree. I have found the best approach is to create a sample of what you intend to do before you approach them. Place their logo and name prominently above the content and utilize some of their design elements. Not only does this provide them a reason to work with you, it allows you to leverage the equity of their brand. Most important, always, ALWAYS obey copyright laws, and always get the authors' written permissions to use their content.[12]

Content Sharing Models

Although most sites find they quickly create a hybrid of the following models, most content agreements fall within three basic models. These are:

- Co-branded areas
- Content shares and trades
- Imbedded link trades

Each of these models relies on some form of barter. Most likely you will find yourself trading content for traffic or trading content for content. When you begin this process, always make sure your Web site remains the point of reference. This means your consumer should always return to your site as the source for their information. If you are not sure of this, ask where the consumer would go if you changed content partners. If the consumer is more likely to go to your partner's site, they are the point of reference. Although I am an advocate of long-term partnerships, the Internet changes quickly as do alliances. If your site is not the point of reference, you risk losing your position. If that happens you can find yourself becoming little more than a tool to drive traffic to another site.

Co-branded Content Area

The first type of shared content model is the co-branded area. This is the easiest to create and the most prolific. It is a very good way to increase the content offered by your site without having to develop the content itself.

---

[12] A note on copyright laws: Aside from the legal aspect and threat of legal action, it took someone time and money to create that content. Yes, the Internet works on the concept of sharing content, but sharing does not mean stealing.

In this model, your site creates a content area using another site's data or information. This area will most likely contain your partner's logo and possible references within the text referring to the other site as the creator of the content.[13]

In this model, the hosting site gains content it would otherwise not have, and the partner site gains increased awareness from its logo placement and additional traffic through the various links. When developed properly, it creates a win-win situation and opportunities for mutual growth.

Depending on the content being traded, co-branded agreements can be created between Web sites, television stations, newspapers, magazines, or any other content provider. There is no reason to limit this strictly to Internet companies. In fact, in many cases it is almost best not to limit it to Internet companies. Offline media can often provide a more widely known brand and a greater opportunity to reach a larger audience.

In some ways creating a co-branded content partnership is like selling advertising. Your ability to create a partnership depends on your ability to deliver the audience your partner wants to receive, so make sure you have your traffic and audience numbers available before you approach another site.

Content Shares and Trades

Content share areas are similar to co-branded areas. Instead of trading content for traffic, one content package is traded for another content package. Both sites benefit by adding content to their site that they would otherwise not have, and by the ability to drive traffic through the links each site receives. A content share is a very good way to add content to your site and to generate traffic through the links from your partner's site.

Again, the key to a successful share or trade is to be able to revise your partner's content to fit into the overall look and feel of your Web site. The goal to a share is not only to increase the amount of content you are offering, but also to increase the amount of content consumers attribute to your site—not to your partner's site. The best way to accomplish this is by offering to do the work. Most sites will gladly accept if you offer to create the content areas. It lessens their workload. It also allows you to dictate the design elements. Just don't get greedy. There is a fine line between incorporating your brand into a shared area and creating a mini-site.

---

[13] Referrals to this include "Content created by [Company Name]" or "Created in conjunction with [Company Name]."

Imbedded Links

The final type of content share is found within imbedded link trades. In this model, the host Web site creates a link to another Web site allowing the consumer a quick path to that information. This is probably the least desirable type of share because it sets up the partnering site as the point of resource. Should the consumer want that information again, they will likely visit the partner site directly rather than travel through the host site.

However, there is no reason a series of imbedded links cannot be created at first and revised as time permits. Just remember to allow yourself the opportunity to do so when you are creating your agreements.

Assessing Your Resources

Depending on what you want to do on the Internet, you can spend anywhere from several hundred to several million dollars developing an online presence. If you are not experienced designing and creating online content, hire someone who is. Almost every successful online businessperson I interviewed knew what their strengths were. They also realized building a Web site was not one of them. The different standards in browsers, servers, bandwidth, programming, and design functions make it almost impossible for one person to create an online presence that works. It takes people from a number of different fields. I have found those people are best found in a company whose core strengths lie in designing and building Web sites.

Yes, there are packaged programs that will help you create a Web presence. However, with most of these programs, the elements that make them easy to use do so at the cost of compatibility. They do not easily accommodate the various browser technologies. This means what you see is not necessarily what your customer sees and may not even function on your customer's browser.

I have learned the pitfalls of trying to create a Web site firsthand. Avoid my mistakes and bring in an outside person. If it requires picking up the telephone and describing your project to an online design firm, do it. Present them with an outline of your plan and get an idea of what it will take to build it. If you cannot afford to pay someone, consider creating a partnership based on a profit-share. The highly successful Bluefly.com did this and was able to create a site that far exceeded its expectations. Depending on the project, there are many smaller design firms or independent designers and programmers that will work on a percentage of potential revenue.

Graphic design and site design; HTML, Java, and flash programming; database creation and maintenance; server upkeep—all of these are elements to be considered when developing a site. If you are unfamiliar with some of them, bring in somebody who isn't. Realize what your capabilities are and understand the limits of your resources and work within them.

As a businessperson your job is to create a business plan that works and ensure the proper elements are in place to make it successful. Your job is not to micromanage every element of your online presence. To do so is to doom yourself to failure. There are simply too many elements for one person to do it all.

Choosing and Working with a Design Shop

After you have developed a direction for your site and determined what you want, there is a good chance you will decide to hire an outside firm to bring your ideas to life. If you do, your goal is to create a box within which your developer will work. This means outlining the content, design, and interactivity you want on your site. Once that is done, you will want to find a designer or developer that mirrors the look and feel you are trying to create.

Do not look for someone who has created similar Web sites. Look for the one who has developed the Web site you want. When you have found a number of designers you think you might want to work with there are several questions you will want to ask and be ready for.

The first question you have will most likely be cost. To assess costs, you will need to have a list of components you want on your site. Look at other sites. See what they have done. Build a list of URLs and note the functionality you want incorporated into your site. Send this list to several developers in order to get several bids for the project.

Some designers will charge by the hour. Others will charge by the project. The best way to compare these costs is to have potential developers create a menu that prices each element out separately. By doing this, you will be able to assess the value of each component and determine which is essential and which should be viewed as added value. At the same time, if the developer wants to create additional elements, this allows you to assess their value in real terms.

Since the Web changes frequently, and because small design changes can create large cost differences, most developers are reluctant to work for a flat fee. If they insist on working on an hourly basis, protect yourself by having them prepare low, expected, and high cost estimates. By doing this, you will know the project will not cost less than the lowest, but that it will not exceed the highest cost presented.[14]

Just as important as the cost is the willingness of the designer to work with you to create your vision. Often times it's better to hire a smaller shop that will put in the time and energy your project will require. Free consultations, changes in design, and the ability to incorporate additional elements will all add up to a better site. Make sure your designer is willing to work with you, not the other way around.

Determine ahead of time what elements you will need to provide and which the designer will create. Will you need to supply text, graphics, and other elements? Will you need to purchase a license for the use of specific elements or are the costs included in the budget? The creation of Real Video files for a site is one thing. Buying a license to use them is another. Make sure all the elements your designer implements into the site include all the licenses required.

File format and delivery systems should also be determined ahead of time. If you plan on creating graphics and delivering them to your designer, make sure you are both working on the same platform; otherwise, there will be problems. Make sure you iron them out in advance.

Make sure your developer is willing to help set up your site and ensure its functionality. Designing is one thing. Making it work is another. Murphy's law prevails on the Internet. If necessary, write in a cost for consulting after the site has launched. There will invariably be problems regarding compatibility issues. Having the developer available for questions will save a lot of time and money in the long run.

Finally, determine specific deadlines for all elements of a project. Have the developer create a calendar if necessary and even incorporate late penalties if the project is on a time constraint. If your customers expect to see something at a specific time, they will not care who your developer is. They will only care why it is not available. Not only will this ensure the developer meets your timeline, it will ensure they commit fully to the project.

CREATING A COMMUNITY

Community is an Internet term for building a strong relationship with and among users of a Web site or other online presence. An online com-

---

[14] If you're curious what Web designers and programmers make, you may want to visit *http://www.planetx.org/~jenn/producers/salary.html*. This is a list of links for stories and surveys related to all types of Web jobs.

munity is based around a group of consumers who share a common interest or goal. A Web presence that is able to create a sense of community not only creates a stronger relationship with its customer, but has a better foundation from which to conduct business.

As you may imagine, the ability to create a community comes back to content. According to a 1998 Forrester Research report, content is what drives 75 percent of consumers to return to their favorite sites. With this in mind, it should be of no surprise that an online presence that responds to the consumer's needs, enables the consumer to interact with the content and other consumers, and even enables the consumer to create content themselves is more likely to maintain the consumer's interests.[15] By moving beyond informational content and creating relational content, almost any Web presence can begin to create community and develop what is known as stickiness.[16]

Moving beyond an informational Web site and creating a community is the gray area where marketers become publishers and publishers become marketers. For some it is a confusing and difficult concept to grasp. But it is really very simple. Both successful online marketing and publishing require listening to the consumer and responding to their needs. Building a community requires both the publisher and the marketer to forgo immediate benefits in order to create content for the sole purpose of appeasing the customer. Building communities and increasing stickiness are the results of accomplishing this.

Starting a Community Pre-Launch

For ease of writing, this section will assume the creation of a Web site. However, the rules apply to almost any Web presence being developed.

The process for creating a community starts during the development process of an online presence. Every person and every business has a choice very early on. They can either create a presence of their own design, and hope their customers likes it when it is complete, or they can bring their customers into the design process and develop a presence the customer has already said they like.

At this point, there really is no right way to proceed. If you have a fairly simple Web site it may be easier and less expensive to create a Web

---

[15] An excellent book that covers the value of online community is *Net Profit* by John Hagel III and Arthur Armstrong.

[16] The concept of stickiness is covered more completely in the section titled The Ongoing Marketing of a Site.

site and then revise it after your customers have a chance to make comments. If your presence is more complex and more expensive, you may want to include your customer in the design process. This will require more time, but at least you will know your site or email program is what your customer wants. Again, the choice is largely dependent on the size and complexity of the online presence you want to create.

There are numerous ways to get the consumer involved in your Web presence and allow them some sense of ownership over the content. However, at this stage your goal should be twofold: First, to collect as much information as possible as to what your customer wants to see on your Web site, and second, to collect email addresses so that you can market your site and generate interest. Three examples that will allow you to do this include:[17]

- Holding informal focus groups, you can have the consumer help you design an interface they respond to.
- Creating an email newsletter prior to the launch of your site that will allow you to generate interest and test ideas that most interest your customers.
- Developing a promotional sweepstakes you can gather customer information and test basic site plans.

Drawing Attention with a "Coming Soon" Page

Regardless of which direction you decide to take it is essential to create an initial Web page even before your site launches. This allows you to preface the site you are building and also allows you to capture names and possible participants.

The easiest way to achieve this is to create a "coming soon" page. A "coming soon" page helps to promote a site by giving visitors a chance to see what will appear after the launch. It also enables to research various elements, which will initiate interaction with future customers. If you have several designs or site options that you are unsure of, your "coming soon" page can request visitors help test the various site designs by joining a focus group or other research element. It can also offer participation in a newsletter to disseminate pre-site information.

All of this requires a response mechanism. This can be as simple as a link to a page with various thumbnail site designs and a series of but-

---

[17] More information on research can be found in the section titled Research tools.

tons to allow testing, or a sign-up box for an email program. This can even include an invitation for participation in an online focus group or other research element.

Creating the foundation for an online community is not difficult, but it does require the creation of an initial page and some form of response mechanism. Once created, almost any idea or concept can be tested easily and inexpensively, and some level of excitement can be created by an ongoing series of simple and short updates as to the site's progress.

However, do not expect to drive thousands or even hundreds of consumers to your pre-site presence unless you are able to promote it. Aside from the promotional tools listed in this book, an easy way to start the process is to send an email to your friends and business associates announcing your focus groups, questionnaires, newsletters, or sweepstakes. Ask them to participate and pass the email on to others.

Use bulletin boards on other sites to announce your design tests and sweepstakes, or list them in other email newsletters or newsgroups. Use whatever method you wish, or combine those listed in this book, but consumers will not respond to what they don't know exists. It is never too early to begin promoting your site, and the traffic you drive before it is up will multiply once it is launched.

Focus Groups and Bulletin Boards

As you will find in the research section of this book, focus groups allow you to capture a great deal of information about a site's design and navigation. For the most part, this requires using a moderated chat engine and posing a series of questions to the participants. Because it is real time, it allows the moderator to follow a line of questioning as it evolves, enabling them to delve deeper into potential issues. Although more expensive than other forms of research, creating and using online focus groups will probably result in the most complete research results.

Newsletter

An email newsletter accomplishes three objectives. It allows the site to capture email addresses, it provides the site with a tool to test respondents, and it helps to generate interest in the site.

In a way, a pre-site newsletter is much like a movie preview. It will contain excerpts from the site and offer teasers for the upcoming content. The objective is to create excitement about what the site will hold. It should provide useful information and also allow recipients to voice their own opinions and needs.

Although it should not be overly promotional, a pre-site newsletter is one of the best tools to generate interest and develop the foundation of a community by building a list of consumers interested in a particular topic and allowing them some ownership over the site's development. This is easily accomplished by incorporating questions about what recipients want to see in a site, or even directing them to sample pages for their responses. A newsletter can bring recipients into the site development process over a longer period of time.

Remember, this newsletter is being used to promote the upcoming site. It is not intended to be a stand-alone program, and should only run for a month or so, lest the consumer lose interest. This type of newsletter will commonly contain excerpts from a site and offer teasers for the content coming soon. Much like a movie trailer, the newsletter should be designed to create excitement about what the site will hold. That means it should provide useful information and not be overly promotional or you will lose future visitors quickly.

Sweepstakes

Similar to the newsletter, if you want to generate interest and capture some information, connect a sweepstakes to your "coming soon" page. This can be as simple as a product giveaway, or it can be incorporated into a survey asking demographic or other information. It can even be used as an inducement for consumers to vote on design options. Regardless of how the sweepstakes is used, make sure the winners are announced on the day the site is launched. After all, why waste a chance at driving traffic on your first day?

Micro-sites

There are many Web sites that allow and encourage you to create an online community within their systems. Geocities, Excite, and Fortune City are just some of them. Their businesses are built around the concept of people developing and managing their own content using their systems for free.

As you develop your content, it is a fairly simple process to locate an appropriate section in which to place your content and begin drawing interest from online consumers. Again, rather than providing all your content, use your content as a teaser to develop user interest, capture email addresses, or start an online newsletter.

Depending on your success, when it comes time to launch your site, you can either fold your existing micro-site into your new Web site, bringing your customers with you, or continue maintaining it as a tool to further drive traffic.

Building a Community Post Launch

Building a community means finding a common interest shared by your customers. It means providing them with a way to voice their opinions and a way for you to respond to them. It means creating a two-way conversation between your site and your customers and between your customers themselves. You are, in effect, creating an online coffee shop in which customers can interact with you behind the counter and other customers in the shop.

There are several elements common to any online community that we will discuss. These include, but are not limited to:

- An identifiable content area that targets a particular interest
- Some level of exclusivity
- A resource of information customers can rely on
- The ability to interact with other consumers
- Access to general information gathered by the site

Identifiable Content Areas

Communities thrive on knowing there is some level of exclusivity. Gated communities exist in almost every city of the world. Private clubs thrive on being able to provide special benefits to their members. Buyers' clubs help establish loyal customers built on the exclusivity of having purchased a specific product. What each of these has in common is a doorway, a way for members of the community to know they have arrived.

One of the first steps in creating an area of interest is to build a doorway to it. On the Internet a doorway can be a button customers click to enter or a path identified on the navigation bar. Either way, without this, the information is available to the general public and there is no sense of exclusivity.

As you may have guessed, a doorway limits the number of members. The exclusivity that creates a community also limits its size. Greater exclusivity means fewer members and less traffic, but theoretically traffic of greater value. It is a catch-22, but one with a solution.

By creating a Web site that includes general information that will appeal to a larger audience, and developing specific content areas with

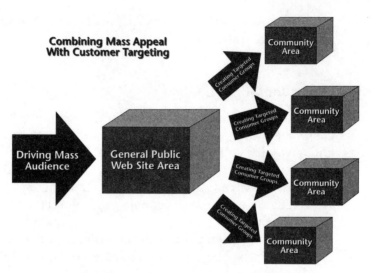

Combining Mass Appeal with Customer Targeting

detailed resources from that, an online presence can be created that both drives traffic and targets the needs of specific individuals.

Clubs and Exclusivity

One of the best ways to create smaller communities within a single Web presence is to create a series of clubs or members only areas. This will require some form of registration on the member's part. The goal of this registration is to better ensure entrants will be truly interested in the community's subject matter. In addition, a registration process that captures member information creates a series of benefits for the site, its members, and potential advertisers.

For its members, benefits of joining a club include:

- Avoiding the mass audience of the Web
- Ability to contact and trade information with others sharing their interests
- A more direct path to the information they seek

For online publishers, benefits of creating a club include:

- Ability to track member movements and interests
- Greater knowledge of who their customers are
- More direct communication with members

For online advertisers, benefits of advertising in a club are:

- More targeted demographic with which to market
- Ability to target members based on specific interest
- Greater control over where advertising is placed and who sees it

By its very nature, a club or members-only area creates a very targeted group of people interested in a specific subject. Not only does a club provide an exclusive area for its members, it also provides an excellent opportunity to bring advertisers and their customers together in an ad-friendly environment. By creating sponsorship opportunities that offer members access to the products and services they want at a discount, publishers can easily develop an online commerce area that benefits members (discounted products) and advertisers (a pre-qualified customer base).

A book club is an excellent example of this. If an online publisher creates a Web site for book lovers, they could create a general section with book reviews and the opportunity to purchase books. However, they could also create specific book clubs for biographies, history, romance, and mysteries. Each of these would provide sample chapters from select books, chats with favorite authors, sweepstakes to win books or trips, and sneak peeks at upcoming books.

Because the online publisher is able to deliver a specific type of book lover, they can then approach book publishers and sell opportunities for upcoming authors to promote their books through the same chats, sweepstakes, and sneak peeks members enjoy. As you can see, an online club can quickly build revenue opportunities because of its ability to deliver a very targeted audience. If that opportunity is developed correctly, the publisher, the advertiser, and the members benefit through content with an added value attached.[18]

Registration

For the member, a registration process that suggests some form of exclusivity will better help to ensure they can escape the jungle of the mass Web audience. At its most basic, registration requires the creation of a member name (usually an email address) for the person to identify him- or herself with. At a higher level a password can be added to ensure

---

[18] For more information on creating and selling sponsorships, see section titled Preparing Your Site to Profit.

some level of security, or a cookie can be incorporated to enable instant member recognition.

As with any online questionnaire or entrance requirements, the amount of information a member is willing to give up will be directly related to the perceived value of becoming a member. At first, do not pry too deeply. Work to develop your membership numbers with an easy entrance process. As your membership grows, continue asking questions and increase your database slowly. Trying to find out everything at first will leave you with very few members.[19]

An example of a basic registration process can be found on *The New York Times'* Web site. Here, a simple process is used to register readers. Once registered, they can then read the publication online. In return, *The New York Times* has information that helps it sell more targeted advertising. An example of a more complex registration process can be found on the Webpersonals Web site. Here a complete user information questionnaire is completed and a user name with password is used each time the member wants to enter. Both of these examples gather just enough information to serve their purposes, but provide entrants with a benefit to justify the level of questions asked.

Interaction

One of the most important elements of a community is the ability for members to interact. The more interaction members have with each other, the greater sense of community they will have, and the more likely it will be that they will return again and again.

As the host of a community, your job is to facilitate a conversation among the members and provide as many ways as possible for them to interact. Although any of a web site's components can stand alone, connecting them together creates an ongoing conversation that continues from email to bulletin board to chat. It will build a stronger community and a better presence that members will want to return to. For instance, announcing the creation of a bulletin board in response to a question on an email newsletter not only provides members with an additional way to communicate, it continues a current topic of conversation. It's like taking a conversation away from the dinner table and into the den for coffee. It keeps the party going.

---

[19] Additional information on developing and maintaining research programs may be found in chapter 6, Research and Customer Service to Enhance Communication.

Some elements include:

Newsletters

Creating interaction among members can include any number of elements. Email newsletters are usually the easiest to implement and control. These are regular emails (daily, weekly, or monthly) that follow one topic and encourage members to post responses via email. The person running the newsletter has control over which emails are included and which are edited. Not only does this maintain the focus of the newsletter, but ensures responses retain some semblance of decorum.

Bulletin Boards

Bulletin boards can be incorporated into almost any Web presence. They allow members to pose questions directly to other members and enable those members to respond. If there is a fear some members may misbehave, bulletin boards can be monitored. Here, each response is sent to a central location at which point they are reviewed before being posted. Although this does take additional work, it ensures the content remains in focus.

To help ensure member interaction, it is best to give bulletin boards a reason for them to exist. Providing a product review and asking for member comments is a good place to start generating interest. Creating an ongoing story for people to add to is an adaptation of the basic bulletin board and another way to generate interest.

However, a bulletin board on its own will usually languish unless its readers are given a reason to participate. If hiding a bulletin board behind another element, such as an ongoing story, will add to participation, do it.

Chat

At one point, chat seemed like an incredible way to put people in touch with each other. However, boys will be boys and girls will be girls, and chat has a tendency to bring out the worst in people. Today, there are a number of programs to enable people to communicate easily and without disruption. However, it is usually not the software people are wary of. As if this weren't enough, unless there is a large user audience (e.g., Yahoo!) to appeal to, running a chat for 24 hours a day is expensive and usually fails to bring people simply because they don't log on at the same time. A chat with ten participants is less than interesting.

If you want to create a chat to bring your customers together, think about creating an online event and monitoring it. This means hosting a chat event that runs for a specific time period and hopefully is attached to a well-known personality. An author chat held between 6 P.M. and 8 P.M. that enables his or her fans to talk is an example of such an event. Enabling fans to talk to a sports personality just after a game is another. Bringing together interior designers to talk about the Bauhaus movement is yet another.

Holding events rather than general chats achieves several things. It gives members a reason to log on at a specific time, it centralizes the chat on a particular subject, and it maintains the focus on a particular subject. Similar to bulletin boards, if there is no impetus to begin chatting about a subject, there are too many directions for the chat to take, and all it takes is one person to sidetrack things.

Similar to monitoring a bulletin board, having all chat postings go through a central monitor will slow down the chat a bit, but it will ensure the conversation maintains some level of decorum. If the chat is limited to an hour or two, monitoring the chat usually will only require one additional person and will help to ensure success.

Polls

Members are just as curious as you are about who their fellow members are. Providing them with that information not only lets them know who else is in their club, it gives them an incentive to provide more information. This does not mean providing individual email addresses or individual information. It does mean providing general information, such as average age, gender, type of employment, areas of interest, or reaction to current events via polls.

Providing this type of information further brings members together and helps them know who the others in their community are. Asking a yes or no question every week about a current event or policy and then posting the results is a good way to bring members back each week. It can also lead into a bulletin board for those members wanting to continue the conversation.

Affinity Programs

Almost everybody is looking for some sort of added value. For a member, this means receiving exclusive benefits. Depending on the subject of the club, a great deal of value can be created through affinity programs. The ability to create an affinity program is usually dependent on the number of members a club has. However, affinity-style benefits can be created for clubs of almost any size.

The process of creating a program is fairly simple. It requires contacting companies with products or services that appeal to members and offering them access to your member base in exchange for product discounts. The value of having direct access to 10,000 book lovers is worth the cost of offering a discount to most booksellers.

Examples of such programs can be found on the American Bar Association's Web site, located at www.aba.org, or at the StudentAdvantage Web site, located at www.studentadvantage.com. Both offer their members specific benefits that not only increase the value of being a member but also provide a way for select companies to promote their products.

With each of these examples, it is important that you retain control of how and when member services are promoted. You do not want to anger your members by allowing your affinity partners to send large amounts of junk mail directly to members. However, this can be avoided by having all contact with your members go through a specific mail house, or only allowing you to send email to them.

Content Creation

Most Web sites view member-created content as out of their reach. It is perceived as too much work to provide members with this capability, then to have to monitor each one. This is a lot of work; however, member-created content does not have to start with member-created Web sites.

The goal of a true community is to create a place where members can interact with each other and develop their own content according to their own needs. When successful, this means the host of the Web site provides the impetus for members to speak to each other, and then provides some level of monitoring to ensure the conversation stays focused.

Member-created content can start with posting humorous emails sent in by members; it can include member reviews of products. It can be a list of restaurant reviews. It can be hints from members on dealing with local tax laws. As its name implies, member-created content is simply content that members create. It does not have to be interactive. It does not have to be instantaneous. All it has to be is from the members.

Intuit has created a very effective small business Web site. It has a number of areas in which members provide each other with tips and hints on running a small business. What Intuit has done is create an opportunity for members to help each other. It has ended up with an almost endless amount of content, most of which was created by its members.

CONCLUSION

Creating content is essential to creating an online presence. Creating branded content is essential to creating a successful online business. There is simply too much competition on the Internet, and it is far too easy for the consumer to access it to try to start an online business without developing content that addresses the consumer's needs quickly and easily.

In today's rapidly changing world of marketing, to be successful an online business cannot risk losing one element in the battle for the consumer's attention. The only way to ensure a win is to brand every inch of a Web presence and the content within it. It also means continually moving forward, from developing an informational presence to a relational presence. Yes, this means every online marketer reaches a point when they become an online publisher. However, this never means forgetting the rules of basic branding.

The only thing worse than losing a customer because you failed to provide them with the information they were looking for, is losing them because they couldn't remember where they found it. The only way to prevent that from happening is to create a memorable brand that resonates throughout your presence.

CHAPTER FOUR

Driving Traffic and Keeping It in Your Online Store

"If you build it, they will come." This is probably the worst saying that ever invaded the Internet mindset. Believe it at your own peril.

Like any brick-and-mortar store, you can have the hottest site with the best information and most graphically appealing design on the Web and still get no traffic. Unless a Web site is actively and consistently promoted, few are likely to find it and even fewer are likely to remember it. With thousands of competitors, it's far too easy to become lost in the electronic haystack.

So how do you develop an audience into a loyal following? The same way stores and magazines have been doing it for years: By creating a consistent message and delivering it to your target audience. The only difference is on the Internet, the tools need to be different. Once again, it is not the wheels that have changed, it's the cart.

In this section we will outline the strategies for promoting a new Web site and for maintaining the promotions of an existing Web site. However, both strategies deal with some basic concepts of how a consumer interacts with the content of a Web site.

Consumers who are not just surfing around are on the Internet to look for specific information. They link to specific content within a site because that is exactly what they want. Less and less do consumers link to a home page; rather they link to specific content that is of interest to them. That is exactly what should be promoted—the benefits the consumer can find on the site, not the site itself. Yes, all the advertising should follow the brand images that have been established, but they should promote specific benefits.

To market on the Internet, it is essential to keep in mind what is being marketed. It is not the Web site, it is the content within it. It is the content the consumer is after. It is the content that promotes the product. Effective marketers do not promote a Web site; they promote the content within it.

In general, promoting a Web site is no different than promoting a store or product. It means creating a consistent message and sending it out to the most likely customers. On the Internet, some steps would include:

- Register your site with the most popular directories and search engines such as Yahoo!, Lycos, and Alta Vista.
- Purchase or trade banner advertising with other sites.
- Create links with other Web sites that are non-competitive and share a common consumer.
- Develop micro-sites that other Web sites can host.
- Promote your Web site into existing advertisements, press releases, literature, letterheads, and business cards.
- Tell everyone you do business with from customers to suppliers about your Web site and the benefits it will provide them.

First, this book will not cover offline advertising. The creation and maintenance of a traditional advertising campaign that includes print, radio, television, and outdoor advertising is worthy of a complete aisle in any bookstore. Suffice it to say, offline advertising has proven to be extremely effective in driving consumers online. If you doubt this, look into the launch of the Victoria's Secret Web site. Yes, the content attracted consumers, but without the offline promotions they would never have responded so quickly and with such enthusiasm.

At the very least, know that your Web address should be included on any offline advertising. URLs are now a staple part of almost every television commercial, print ad, and radio spot. They are also included on business cards, flyers, letterheads, and brochures of companies large and small. To refrain from including your Web site in your offline promotions means your vendors, suppliers, and business associates will either not know about your Web site, or will not consider it important enough to visit.

THINKING OUTSIDE THE WEB SITE BOX

Brand Driven, Results Oriented

To be successful, online advertising must extend your brand beyond your Web presence which means it needs to maintain the look and feel of your brand. At the same time, it must drive traffic back to your content, which means it needs to produce results: Brand driven—results oriented.

Like any traditional advertising campaign, you will need to combine a number of elements into one coordinated campaign that extends the online brand and either a) delivers branded content to your customer, or b) drives pre-qualified consumers back to your branded content or product.

Contrary to what some media buyers think, the best way to achieve this is not through a campaign of banner ads, but by leveraging the content you have already created. How to do this? By constructing teasers in the form of micro-sites and sponsorships, and supporting them with other online advertising tools

Extending the URL

Too many people have created Web sites in order to get out of the box of traditional advertising only to fall into the URL box. Instead of creating a Web site and trying to draw consumers into it, why not deliver your content directly to your customers? After all, it should not matter whether someone visits your URL. It should matter if someone buys your products or pays you for advertising. A Web site is not an advertisement; it is a medium to deliver your content.

Think about a $10,000 banner ad campaign. If you spend that $10,000 on banner ads and receive a 2 percent click-through rate (click-through rates commonly average 1 percent–3 percent) you are losing $9,800 worth of advertising. However, if you spend $10,000 hosting a page of content on another site, everyone that clicks on your page reads your content. This results in 100 percent effectiveness. By including multiple text links or a purchase opportunity, this increases your chance of driving traffic and closing sales. Similarly, if consumers read your content and like what they see, they will follow your links—but to do this, they have to see more than just a banner ad.

Reflect the Brand

All online advertising is a component of the overall marketing campaign and an extension of your Web site; as such it needs to reflect the elements already reflected in your brand. However, this does not mean each ad has to promote the same thing. Each can and should leverage a specific aspect of your branded content in order to target a very specific consumer.

In traditional advertising, Mercedes may advertise in a car magazine, touting the quality of its engine, while advertising in a luxury magazine, touting the quality of its design and interiors. Both ads promote the same element—quality, yet both focus on the quality that will best attract the audience to which they are advertising.

Online advertising is no different. All online advertising should reflect the established brand and support a given product's position in a way that targets the interests of a specific consumer—and what better way to do this than through content.

THE INITIAL STEPS IN MARKETING A WEB SITE

Whether your Web site was created to promote a product, build a brand, or supply information, the first steps to promoting it are similar. Getting a primary placement with the search engines and directories is one of the most important elements. These are the primary tools consumers use to find content. The higher up your Web site appears, the more traffic they will drive to your content.

After a search engine listing, promoting your site is very similar to promoting almost any other product or service offline. It requires an ongoing campaign of advertising and public relations that creates a consistent message for your audience. The primary difference lies in the tools you use to communicate your message to your audience. The level each component is used depends on the Web site and its resources. Some components may be used initially and some initiated later on depending on the type of Web site and its resources.

Search Engine/Directory Placement

There are two types of search tools on the Internet—search engines and directories. Both are considered the Yellow Pages of the Internet. The primary difference is a directory (e.g., Yahoo!) uses a human to look at various Web sites, while a search engine (e.g., Hotbot.com, Altavista.com) uses programs called robots or spiders that actually visit specific Web pages and assess each based on the number of times a specific word appears. Because of this, search engines can research more Web pages in less time and will often return more Web pages that may or may not be relevant to your search.

Because directories (e.g., Yahoo!) use humans to look at Web sites and assess where they should be placed on their listings, they can often provide a more targeted result based on an actual review.

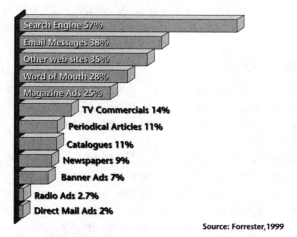

Source: Forrester,1999

Most Frequently Used Sources for Finding
Online Content

There are new search engines coming out that combine the two search techniques. These usually return a result that includes both a large number of sites with some level of relevancy with a list of preferred sites that have been researched by humans.[20]

Regardless, the process for the user is simple. The user types in a keyword related to their search and the search engine searches through a database of Web sites, listing each by its relevancy to that keyword.

Basic Rules to Announcing Your Site

Timing

The best time to announce your Web site is not the day it is published. Wait a day or two after it is completed so that you can test all the links. There is nothing worse than finding dead or misdirecting links after people start arriving. Additionally, because it will take anywhere from a day to several weeks for the search engines to process the information, do not expect instant results. Above all, be sure not to list your site with

---

[20] A listing of the primary search engines can be found in appendix 1.

search engines before it is published. It is very difficult for a search engine to spider a site effectively that contains bad or missing data.

What to List

At first list all the primary pages of your Web site. This includes the home page and all the main section pages. As you have more time, continue listing the remaining pages. Yes, you do want all the pages of your Web site to appear. The more pages you have listed, the more likely someone is to click on your page. Further, as the content changes from page to page, the search engines will include your site in more and more searches. Rather than just having your site pop up when someone types in the Keyword "pet," it could also pop up when someone types in "cats," "dogs," "mice," and "guinea pigs."

As more information is added to your site, you will want to resubmit your Web site to all of the search engines and directories. It is best to set up a regular schedule to do this on at least a quarterly basis and more often if your data changes daily, weekly, or monthly, or when you are announcing a new section.[21]

Listing Tools

Today there are a number of tools that allow you to list your site quickly and easily. One such tool is located at *www.submitit.com*. Although some of their services cost money, most provide an easy method of manual submission. If you do not want to pay a service to list your site, it will mean taking the time to do it yourself.

A good way to find how your site is listed is through SubmitIt!'s positioning agent located at *www.positionagent.com*. This reports where your Web site is currently ranked in the leading search engines for your selected keywords. Not only will this tell you when to revise your listing, it will allow you to boost low listings with an ad buy or determine which metatags to revise.

A second Web site to use is *www.webgarage.com*. This site performs a quick analysis of your site and assesses its ability to work with various browsers and search engines. Not only will it tell you how well your site's metatags will do, it will tell you how compatible your site is for different browsers and connections.

---

[21] A fantastic site for search engine information is maintained by Danny Sullivan at *http://www.searchenginewatch.com/*

Metatags and Tricks

What is a metatag? At the top of almost every Web page is a series of HTML lines. They are denoted by the word metatag—hence the name. Originally, a metatag was a way for a programmer or designer to make notes to themselves and to other designers. At first this included the title of a page, a brief description of that page, and some information about the programming itself.

Realizing these were the keys to finding information about a particular Web page or Web site, search engines created small programs (spiders) to look for keywords on a particular Web page. The more words a Web site had about a particular subject, the more relevancy that site had to a particular search and the higher the search engines would list it. Once Webmasters realized this, they began placing words on their sites to increase their prominence in these listings, and thus began the search engine wars.

Webmasters found ways to increase their listings while search engines created ways to separate legitimate words from promotional words. Unless you have the time to constantly update and revise your metatags, create an accurate one and leave it alone until your Web site changes enough to warrant a new one.

Using Metatags

If a particular page does not have a metatag, they are losing traffic. There are three basic metatags that you should be concerned with—title, description, and keywords. For the most part, they appear as described in this section.

The best way to start using metatags is to determine what your competition is doing. To find this out, go to any of the search engines (e.g., Hotbot.com, Altavista.com) and type in a relevant keyword. When the search engine returns its list, click on the top listed Web site that appears to be relevant to your site. Once that Web page has downloaded, move your cursor to your browser's toolbar and click on "view" and then on "source." This will allow you to view their source codes (the HTML codes). At the top of this page will be their metatags. It will most likely look like this:

```
<HTML>

<HEAD>

<TITLE>75 words<TITLE>
```

```
<meta name="description" content="150 words.">
<meta name="keywords" content="150 words">
</head>
```

Look at the words other sites use in the title, description, and keyword areas. While search engines differ in the way they analyze metatags, they all use a formula that ranks the frequency of words on that Web page.

The title metatag should include the title of the particular page in a way that incorporates a limited number of keywords. This should generally be 75 words or less, so instead of writing "CNN," a better title would be "CNN for all your up-to-the-minute news and information needs."

By changing the "title" metatag frequently, visiting spiders will sometimes consider that page a new one. Often this will result in its being listed multiple times, increasing your presence on a search engine.

The description metatag should be less than 150 words. It should contain a full description of your Web page with plenty of keywords incorporated into the text.

The keyword metatag should be less than 150 words. Enter keywords as appropriate, separating each one with a comma.

Choosing Metatag Keywords

Choosing an effective keyword means trying to anticipate what the consumer will look for when searching for a particular subject. To do this, return to the branding exercise and make a list of your consumer benefits. Those are most likely the words consumers will enter into a search engine when trying to retrieve information.

The best way to determine what keyword to use is go to the search engines and type in a keyword. Again, go to the top sites that appear and click on the "view source" link that appears on your browser's toolbar. This will show you the keywords they are using, and is usually a good guide to determine which keywords to include on your Web pages.

Although common words like "fun" may help an entertainment site somewhat, they will not help when someone is looking for a more specific subject. Most people search for a specific subject, using such words as "chess," "jokes," "tropical beaches," or "games." Try to use keywords and phrases that target the key benefits of your site.

In addition, people often use more than single words when searching for a subject. They use phrases such as "tropical beaches," or "Internet games." Mirror these phrases in the keyword section of your metatags.

Finally, unless your name is a brand in and of itself like Xerox or Apple, it makes little sense to list it. The goal is not to promote your company's logo, but to match the way your consumer will search for you. If they will use a word to look for you, use it; if not, don't.

Cases and Tenses

Use upper and lower case fonts at the beginning of important keywords. If someone is searching for the word "President," most search engines will only search for "President" with an uppercase "P." However, if someone uses the keyword "president," most search engines will look for both "President" and "president." Therefore it is often smart to include the upper and lower case versions of important keywords.

Similar to the previous uppercase example, it may make sense to pluralize important keywords. Do this only if you have room, and if it makes sense.

Non-Metatag Words

Search engines often compare the relationship words have to each other in sentences. Rethink the copy on each page and see if you can incorporate keywords into the copy. If you are selling coffee, work the word coffee into the text. Don't go overboard and trade good writing for keyword frequency, but there are often many opportunities to exchange one or two words for a word to which those search engines will respond.

Obvious Mistakes with Keywords

Do not try to hide keywords on your Web site by making them the same color as your Web site's background. Search engines found this secret ages ago and will ignore them.

Do not repeat the same words back to back. Separate them. Many search engines ignore repeat words. It is considered safe to repeat a keyword up to about three times. More than that and you risk a search engine ignoring the word altogether.

Announcing Your Site in Newsgroups

Newsgroups, like the World Wide Web, are an element of the Internet. Each one is similar to a bulletin board where people can leave messages about a particular subject. At one time, newsgroups were a primary reason for going on the Internet, and a leading way to exchange ideas and information, but, like much of the Web, they have gone commercial and are often overloaded with announcements for email scams and businesses hawking their wares. For this reason, they are not as effective as they once were, but they can still drive some traffic.

Today there are tens of thousands of newsgroups covering almost every subject one can imagine, and some that still boggle the mind. Similar to a press release, it is important to target only those newsgroups whose content directly relates to your Web site. If you send out erroneous messages to nonrelevant newsgroups you will quickly find the word spam attached to your efforts and your site. That is not good.

Before trying to post a message, monitor the newsgroup to determine what the general content is, and what the responses are like. If the newsgroup is a listing of commercial postings, it is probably best to ignore it. If the newsgroup has a fairly consistent conversation between its members, begin to add to that conversation with relevant postings.

Relevancy is the key to participating successfully with other members of a newsgroup and to driving traffic to your site. No, you will probably not notice a huge upswing in traffic from your efforts. Traffic will come in gradually, but word of mouth can suddenly build to become a very powerful part of your efforts.[22]

Email and Newsletter Lists

Using email and electronic newsletters to promote a site can be a very effective and efficient way to build awareness and drive traffic. There are email lists for every topic imaginable, and for some that are not. Email messages should only be sent through opt-in lists, in which the recipient has elected to receive the email. Sending unsolicited email or spam is not only harmful to your brand, it will result in a backlash from ISPs, consumers, and others that you most likely want to avoid.

As with newsgroups, make sure your participation in a newsletter is going to be welcome. The only way to ensure that is to monitor several electronic newsletters. You will most likely not be able to submit a blatant promotion of your site, but by adding content that is relevant to the newsletter's message, you will be able to have your site and name included as the author, promoting it to a very targeted audience.

---

[22]DejaNews is the leading search engine for newsgroups. It is located at *www. dejanews.com* and lists newsgroups based on keywords.

The greatest advantage of using an email list is that the Web user has elected to receive the email and is interested in its content. Similar to advertising on a niche Web site, an ad message that responds to the consumer's need for information about a particular subject will draw a response. A general ad that tries to reach everyone will reach no one.

The best way to find an appropriate email list[23] is to sign up for a list and read the emails. Assess using them based on the relevancy of the content. Do not use a list without trying it. Again, advertising on an email list implies you support its content. Make sure you support it before paying for it.

The best email lists focus on one topic and deliver useful information to the reader. The more targeted the list, the better it will allow the advertiser to target the consumer. In addition, most email lists will allow a longer ad message to be run. This means more information can be placed into an email message than on a banner ad, again resulting in a better response.

Issuing a Press Release

Regardless of whether you are targeting online or offline media, a well-written press release can be one of the best tools to driving consumers to your online presence. Regardless of the media, the process is basically the same. Finding the appropriate publication or program to contact, identifying the correct person, finding out what their deadlines and interests are, issuing a press release that responds to their interests, and following the release with a telephone call can help sell the story.

This may sound very similar to the process for marketing a product, because that is exactly what you are doing, only this time your consumers are the writers and editors and your product is your story.[24]

In general, a release should be coordinated with the launching of your site and sent to relevant on- and offline publications that you think will pick it up.[25]

---

[23] Appendix 2 contains resources for finding relevant email lists and information.

[24] Byte, an online publication located at *www.byte.com,* works in a similar manner as the PR Newswire. It allows Web sites to submit news releases for an annual fee. Once listed, that release becomes searchable by all the keywords in the release. Writers and editors are able to use this service to find relevant stories and articles.

[25] More information on writing and issuing a press release can be found in appendix 2.

The Contact

Like the rest of us, writers and editors across the globe use the Internet to access and develop ideas for newsworthy stories. Because of this, the Internet has become an exceedingly easy way to disseminate story ideas to publications and programs of all kind. However, if you think junk email irritates you, just imagine how irrelevant email must irritate an editor. Today, thanks to email and faxes, editors, writers, and producers are inundated with "today's hot story idea." Unfortunately, like the rest of us, each has only a limited amount of space to work with and must choose the most relevant story for their publication or program.

One of the most important elements to a successful public relations campaign is to not send out an endless stream of press releases with the hope that one will hit. More often than not, they will end up in the trash folder. What works is targeting the most appropriate publications and programs and building a relationship with them. A relationship means you know who the proper media contact is, and you know what kind of stories they are seeking. Then, when you write a story, you know it will be of interest to them, and they know you are not going to waste their time.

The Process

Because more people than ever before are using the Internet to find news and information, the Internet has become a gold mine for disseminating press-worthy stories to the general public and to editors.

Many online publications are looking for news stories that will interest their readers and increase their page views. Just like in traditional news media, the online press release remains a source of these stories. By creating newsworthy stories and targeting the appropriate Web sites with them, a smart marketing person can build a buzz that will not only end up on the pages of a Web site, but has the chance of being covered by newspapers, radio, and even television.

You will find that editors and writers know which stories work best for them. This is important. Unless your release is easy to read and quickly grabs their attention with information that piques their interest, it risks getting lost in the shuffle. Again, this means targeting those publications with a direct interest in your story, or it will get no further than the fax machine or email inbox.

A press release is a short story, designed to catch the interest of the editors or writers. If your press release contains a story they think would add to the content of their publication, the editors will usually pick it up and contact you for more information. Whether it is meant for an on- or offline publication, a press campaign starts with the creation of a press release.

A release should fit onto one 8½" × 11" piece of paper and contain a heading with the name of the story and contact information (name, phone number, and email address), followed by the story itself. The story should focus on just one idea or one event (a jack-of-all-stories is the master of none). Trying to fit several ideas into one story will more than likely confuse the editor as to what the story is actually about.

This story should then be sent to appropriate publications through fax, email, or traditional mail. In addition, a newswire should be employed to reach select journalists. PR Newswire and Reuters do more than just provide information to journalists. They feed information to many Web sites including Yahoo! and Lycos which are now reporting on the news. Additionally, mainstream news sites such as CNN, the *Los Angeles Times,* and the *New York Times* continue to be the source of news for consumers and writers alike.

Keep in mind, the larger the news company, the more stories they receive, and the more difficult it becomes to get coverage. Just like marketing a product, start small and expand slowly. Begin with the niche sites that will be more interested in your subject category. Once you begin receiving coverage from smaller publications and Web sites, larger ones are more likely to cover you. Additionally, with online syndication, stories that are covered in some of the niche sites can quickly find their way through journalists to larger news sites.

If you are marketing a beach Web site that sells swimsuits, it would be better to start with smaller beach newspapers or swimwear magazines rather than with a national newspaper like the *New York Times.* Those publications with the most direct interest in your product or your Web site will be the ones quickest to pick up your story simply because your story will more readily appeal to their readers. Editors are no different than the rest of us. They want the story that fits into their publication with the least amount of changes. Even more important, you can avoid having weeks of work quashed by an international crisis or a last minute celebrity scandal.

THE ONGOING MARKETING OF A SITE

Basics of an Online Campaign

Once a site has been introduced, an ongoing promotion campaign is needed to ensure it will continue to drive traffic and remain in the forefront of the consumer's mind.

Fortunately for the advertiser, today's online advertising market is a buyer's market. Due to the increase in Web traffic, the number of available page impressions (advertising inventory) far outnumbers the demand by advertisers. This means Web sites are more willing to drop their prices in order to attract advertisers. Although this will change as more advertisers move their budget onto the Internet, it will not happen quickly. There is simply too much growth.

As a result, prices for advertising have dropped dramatically, which means it is easier today to promote your online presence. With a little negotiating, almost anything can be done for less. However, the key to success remains the same. Finding the most efficient and effective way to spend your money means creating some way to measure the return on investment (ROI).

In advertising, ROI is measured by the cost it takes to reach one thousand consumers (cost per thousand or CPM) and the cost it takes to drive one consumer to your content (cost per click or CPC).

Using the following formulas, anyone can compare different media buys, price structures, and programs using a common pricing model.[26]

Cost per Thousand—CPM

Cost of media buy/number of viewers (in thousands)
$10,000/100,000 = $10,000/100 = $10 CPM

Cost per Click—CPC

Cost of media buy/number of clicks
$10,000/(100,000*2 percent) = $10,000/2,000 = $5 CPC

Both CPM and CPC allow the advertiser to compare different Web sites and even different advertising models. Although these do provide a consistent metric, neither is able to account for the branding element of a Web site. For example, although it is less expensive to advertise in Hotkittendotcom than the *New York Times*, it is probably not the best place for your brand to be seen. Keep this in mind when buying advertising. The value of associating your name with a well-respected brand will increase the value of a specific ad buy that a CPM or CPC calculation will never account for.

---

[26] For beyond-the-banner models, you will have to divide the cost of the sponsorship by the expected page views each sponsored area will receive based on the host site's traffic. This will provide a rough CPM.

Paying Versus Barter

Every site has excess inventory. And as the saying goes, if you can't sell it, trade it. The basic concept is several thousand years old. I give you something, and in exchange you give me something of equal value. On the Internet, the thought goes, why not put impressions that aren't being paid for to use by trading them with another site.

The basic concept of barter arrangements can be as simple as running a banner ad on another Web site while they run their banners on your site. They can be as complex as trading content, logo placements, revenue shares, or any combination of these. For the most part, expect to trade 1:1; that is, one banner for one banner.

When you begin to go into a barter arrangement, start slow. Test the effectiveness of their site and allow them to do the same with yours. It is often best to view a barter relationship as a three-tier program. At the bottom tier is a simple one-to-one banner trade. Tier two may include content trades or sponsorships. Tier three may include co-branding micro-sites and a revenue share. Remember to start off slow; it's always easier to increase a barter arrangement than to stop one.

If a simple banner trade works (tier one), then move on to larger programs that include more elements. Be cautious of putting too much work into a program and a partner that may or may not work out.

As with all other partnerships, find a complementary and noncompetitive Web site and contact its owners. Propose a trade with an opportunity to grow it if it is successful and look to the long term. Not only will this create incentives for your partner; it helps to ensure the long-term goal is not sacrificed for a short-term gain.[27]

General Rules to Online Advertising

Regardless of the advertising model you are using (e.g., banner advertisements, sponsored content, interstitials, advertorials, and email) the following rules apply.

Don't Stop the User Experience, Continue It

Refrain from having your message placed on a Web page that is a step in a process. Users are unlikely to stop in the middle of a process unless the offer is extremely compelling. For example, if a Web site is producing a

---

[27] See appendix 6 for a sample agreement for a basic barter trade.

slideshow, users are not likely to stop watching the show just to click on an ad. Remember—effective online advertising does not stop the user experience, it continues it.

Every Buy Is a Test

Do not buy advertising based on your budget. Buy based on your goals. If you want to get 10,000 visitors and the average click-through rate for the Web is 1 percent, why put all your eggs in one basket? It's better to test several sites so that you learn which ones produce the best results. At a 1 percent click rate, you will need to buy 1,000,000 impressions (10,000/.01) to reach 10,000 visitors. With this in mind, why not buy 100,000 impressions on 10 Web sites, and have the ads on each site link back to a different specific Web page or URL. Next calculate the cost per acquisition from each site. In this way you will be able to track what types of Web sites pull the best results. Those sites that do not perform well do not make the next ad buy.

Expect Performance/Guarantee Results

Set a performance benchmark and follow it. This should be in both CPM and CPC. The CPM guarantees an overall price. The CPC guarantees an ROI. Better still, combine the two to ensure success. A $10,000 ad buy at a $10 CPM with a guaranteed click-through rate of 1 percent means you are guaranteed to not pay more than $10,000. At the same time you are also guaranteed to receive at least 1,000 visitors. This makes the publisher responsible for providing you with a quality advertising vehicle. If a publisher cannot at least deliver the Internet's average click-through rate, it should be the publisher's responsibility to continue producing until they can.

Incentivize the Publisher

Instead of negotiating a CPM, negotiate a click-through rate relative to the CPM. Rather than making a $10,000 ad buy at a $10 CPM, make a $10,000 ad buy at a $10 CPM with a guaranteed 2 percent click-through. If the publisher wants more money (e.g., a $20 CPM) for a guarantee, increase the click-through rate. A $10 CPM with a 2 percent click-through is the same as a $20 CPM with a 4 percent click-through. Advertising on the Web is built around results. Make sure you get them.

Shop Around

You are trying to reach a specific consumer with your ads. Many smaller Web sites that may not be currently serving ads are usually more than happy to place a banner into their design if someone is willing to pay them. An email costs nothing more than two minutes of time, and you will be surprised at the deals you can create. Remember, if you are the only ad on a Web site for an entire month, you own it. That can cause quite a stir if you own ten Web sites in your category, regardless of their size.

Be Careful of Networks

Making a network buy means your ad runs on ALL the sites of a network. The presence of your ad on a Web site implies support of its content. Make sure the sites your ad runs on are sites you want your brand associated with.

Always Ask

There are no fixed prices for Internet advertising. There are no established prices for Internet advertising. I have yet to see a Web site that is 100 percent sold out. Publishers will ask for a higher CPM because they want to get it, not because that is the value of the ad. Ask for a lower price. I have yet to have a Web site say no, flat out. You would be surprised at the prices you may receive quickly and easily.

Places to Advertise

Before looking at the types of online advertising that are available to you, consider the different places in which you can advertise. These primary categories include:

- Search engines
- Niche content sites
- Gateway sites
- Top 100 Web sites
- Local guides
- Networks

Search Engines

Search engines have two basic advertising models—run of site/category purchases and keyword purchases.[28]

Run-of-site (ROS) advertising is run throughout an entire Web site. This is usually the least expensive type of advertising and produces the lowest response rates because it is untargeted. A run-of-category (ROC) ad buy means the advertisement runs throughout a specific section or category. The response rates for a category are usually higher than run-of-site because it allows the advertiser to target a category that matches their demographic profile.

The general thinking is, buying a ROS banner ad reaches a very wide audience, but has a very low click-through rate. More people see the ad. Fewer people respond. Run-of-category advertising costs more, but in delivering a more targeted audience, it will deliver a higher return. Before you buy either, consider how well each will produce and get the account executive to provide some guarantee before you sign an ad buy.

Prices for this can range from $5 CPM on ROS to $50 CPM on ROC, depending on the desirability of the category. Unless you are just trying to drive traffic, consider paying for a category run. There is a level of brand recognition that happens after the consumer sees a particular banner ad multiple times. This will cause them to remember your Web site even after your ad is gone.

A keyword purchase means buying the ad impressions for a specific keyword. When a consumer types in a search word or keyword, your banner ad appears with the results. This is why when you type "vitamins" into Yahoo!, you will probably see a banner ad for Vitaminshoppe.com, Health.com, or any number of other relevant advertisers.

The biggest benefit to a keyword buy is it allows advertisers to target their audience based on a very specific interest or interests. Keywords commonly cost higher (usually starting at a $50 CPM) because of their promise to deliver a better audience and a higher click-through rate.

If you are considering purchasing keywords, the best place to begin your search is with *www.eyescream.com/yahootop200.html*. This is an unofficial listing of the top 200 keywords searched on Yahoo! Although it may not tell your exact keyword, it will provide an estimate for how many impressions a particular keyword can deliver.

---

[28] To find out which search engine to use, refer to appendix 1.

Niche Sites

A second category of Web sites is the niche sites. These are smaller sites that focus on a specific subject and are an excellent way to deliver your ad message to a highly targeted audience. Although these sites will not be able to drive the large traffic numbers of a top 100 site, they will usually perform better in click-throughs. Again, online consumers qualify themselves as an interested consumer every time they click onto a Web site, so if you advertise on a site that attracts a similar consumer, you will most likely receive a better response to your ads. Also, unlike a television or print ad, you are not buying the program's entire audience. You are only buying a specific number of impressions, so it really does not matter how many total page views a site receives. All that matters is that you receive the number you purchased.

Finally, depending on the product being marketed, it may make more sense to advertise on several smaller sites than to spend an entire budget on one larger site. If a volleyball fan visits five different volleyball sites and sees your logo on all of them, they will make a connection. If they see your ad once or twice on a larger sports site, there is little way for them to identify your logo out of the general advertising noise.

One note: Smaller, niche Web sites attract a very targeted audience based on consumer interest. To reach them, create banner ads specific to that subject or to the Web site itself. Mimicking the look and feel of the online publisher means a smoother transition for the consumer and will result in a higher response rate. Running a general interest ad on a niche site will result in a very low response, and an even lower return on your investment.

Top 100 Sites

The top 100 sites, as its name implies, are the largest Web sites ranked by their traffic. The reason for identifying these Web sites is they can often deliver the traffic needed to generate a buzz, and they often carry a greater brand name. Additionally, by advertising on the number ten site, you can probably reach your audience without the higher prices of the top one or two well-known sites. The best way to find a top 100 site is through, you guessed it, *www.100hot.com*.

Local Directories

For some products and services, advertising to the whole world will not make sense. For a restaurant that wants to attract a local consumer who can actually get to a particular store or restaurant, local guides are the best bet.

Leading local guides include *CitySearch, At Hand Network, Sidewalk,* and *DiveIn* to name a few. In addition, almost every local newspaper such as the *Los Angeles Times* and the *New York Times* has created excellent guides that combine local events, shopping, and news. Local newspapers also carry a greater element of branding than most local guides, making them a better way to establish a business or brand.

Depending on the product and target market, local guides and directories are usually better at targeting geographic content than almost any other online content.

Ad Networks

As their name implies, an advertising network brings together a series of Web sites. The largest advantage of working with a network is their ability to deliver a wide range of content quickly and easily. Most advertising networks allow an advertiser to test a number of different sites and then target the best sites producing a higher return. However, this can pose a certain amount of risk.

Sometimes the network's Web sites carry a central theme. Sometimes they do not. Often the Web sites that use a network are those that have trouble selling the ads themselves. Because most consumers view running a banner ad on a Web site as an implicit support of that Web site's content, the advertiser loses some control over where their ad is seen. With the larger networks such as DoubleClick or 24/7, this is not a problem. On the smaller networks, some risk to the brand may be posed.

Elements of an Online Advertising Campaign

Traditional advertising campaigns combine print, television, radio, outdoor, and direct mail to effectively reach their audience. An online campaign is no different. To be effective, an online advertiser should combine banner advertising with various beyond-the-banner elements, press releases, award programs, and promotions to drive traffic and brand the content. Of course, the ability to combine these elements depends greatly on budget, time, and resources. However, with some creativity and persistence a multi-tiered campaign can be created by almost anyone.

As of today, there are no hard and fast rules as to what is possible and what can and cannot be done. Banners, interstitials, advertorials, sponsored content, and logo placement all cross over a very large gray area. There is no hard and true way to combine each element into a campaign. The only correct way to buy advertising is to look at your budget and at your objectives.

Assess every program by its ability to produce results. Assume everything is a test. If something does not perform, refrain from buying it again. There are too many opportunities on the Internet to let someone sell you something that fails to add to your bottom line.

Integrating your traditional marketing and sales programs starts by including your Web site address on your flyers, letterheads, and brochures. If there are advantages to delivering services, programs, or information through your Web site, then provide an incentive in your traditional materials to get customers to go to your site for fulfillment.

The primary elements of online advertising include:

1. Advertisus interuptus
   - Banner advertising
   - Interstitials
2. Content-based advertising
   - Sponsorships and advertorials
   - Micro-sites
   - Email and newsletters
3. Promotions
   - Sweepstakes
   - Offers and Easter eggs
4. Non-Advertising
   - Awards and incentive programs
   - Discussion lists/News group participation
   - OTD: Of the day

Advertisus Interuptus—Banner Advertising and Interstitials

Banner advertising and interstitials are the most common form of online advertising available. Most advertising agencies are comfortable with them because they are easy to quantify. However, both have been producing decreasing results over the past several years. The reason is simple; like the television commercial, the consumer is used to them. They understand why they are there and it is easier to ignore them.

More important, both interrupt the consumer's experience. The value proposition for the consumer says if the content on the other side of the banner is better than the content they are currently viewing, they will click. However, most consumers visit a specific site to see its content, not to go somewhere else.

Although many people like to separate banner advertising from Interstitials, there is really no reason to; they are both purchased based on CPM and their ability to provide a set number of click-through rates. They are both designed to interrupt the consumer's experience and take the consumer to other content. The primary benefit to an interstitial is its size and impact. Because it pops up, it draws more attention. Because it is larger than a 486×60 banner, it can deliver more information. However, what makes the interstitial so full of impact is the exact reason it creates such a backlash. Many consumers do not like their experience interrupted, and this is precisely what an interstitial does.

Both banner advertising and interstitials are bought per impression. One ad impression means your banner ad has appeared when a Web user calls up a Web page. There are a number of ways to track this, but most Web sites use an ad server. This works through a line of HTML code that sits within the design of a Web page. When a user requests a page, the HTML code sends a signal to the ad server to deliver a banner ad. This takes a fraction of a second and the consumer sees a banner ad pop up on the page.

As with all advertising, banner ads are combinations of brand and direct response advertising. For a well-known brand, banner ads can be an inexpensive way to create instant recognition and drive some traffic. For a lesser known brand, banner ads can help drive traffic, but many remain somewhat skeptical of their ability to build a brand.

Content-Based Advertising

Sponsorships and Advertorials

The largest concern with banner ads is that they interrupt the consumer's experience. If a Web site has great content, the consumer is not likely to leave. If the consumer is in the middle of a process, they are even less likely to leave.

Sponsorships are so effective because they allow the consumer to see the advertising message without interrupting their experience. The trick is taking the time to find content that supports your brand and in which your advertising message can be incorporated. If, when sponsoring content you place less emphasis on a blatant ad message and more on integrating your brand into the content, the consumer will be more likely to respond. The better the content, the better the branding, and the more likely the consumer will remember the product.

A good way to ensure higher click-through levels is to combine banner advertising into some form of fixed placement (e.g., content sponsorship or logo placement). Not only does this combination increase the visibility of your brand or product, it allows you to own a particular page and reinforces the consumer's perception of who the content belongs to.

The basic difference between a sponsorship and an advertorial is the producer of the content. Sponsored content is usually created by a publisher rather than an advertiser. Depending on the integrity of the publisher, the content itself is usually considered more reliable by the consumer. Because of this, the consumer places more value on the content. By sponsoring content, usually with a logo placement, the consumer knows the sponsor is, in effect, providing them with the content, which leverages their brand.

An advertorial, on the other hand, is produced by the advertiser, and is usually more blatant about the promotion of their product. Once a consumer realizes they are being advertised to, they are instantly wary of the message. Because advertorials are a more blatant promotion, they will be less believable than a sponsorship.

Micro-Sites

The goal of online advertising is not to drive readers to your Web site, but rather to drive people to your content. As a promotional tool, a micro-site can be one of the best ways to drive qualified traffic to your content or bring your content to the online consumer. If you have a Web site with content, you can create a micro-site.

As a promotional tool, your goal is to find the most compelling content on your site and, in effect, create a teaser for it. The objective is not to provide all of your information to the user. It is to provide just enough to entice them to visit your Web site and your branded content.

More often than not, a micro-site can be part of a larger barter trade. When created with a complimentary and noncompetitive partner, a micro-site will add to the editorial value of your partner's site. By this I mean you are providing content to your partner and they are driving traffic to you.

Creating a Newsletter

All it takes to create your newsletter is to ask people to join and begin sending out your message. The easiest way to do this is to offer visitors to your site a simple sign-up that submits their name to a database.

From there you can ask site visitors to sign up for a newsletter, then distribute it by email. An enewsletter allows you to keep visitors up-to-date on site changes and new offerings. It also serves as a channel for delivering valuable information related to your products that can help convert prospects into customers.

Building Stickiness

Like community, stickiness is an Internet term for a Web presence that is able to build a strong relationship with its customer. Stickiness is the ability to keep a consumer on the site for a longer amount of time. A site that is able to create stickiness enjoys customers who spend a long amount of time on the content, often increasing page counts.

A Web presence that creates stickiness not only creates a stronger relationship with its customer, but is better able to conduct business because the consumer is willing to spend more time on the content. As with community, the ability to create stickiness comes back to content.

This means an online presence that responds to the consumer's needs and enables them to interact with the content and other consumers. When consumers are able to create new content themselves, they are more likely to maintain interest.[29] By moving beyond informational content and creating relational content, almost any Web presence can begin to create community and develop stickiness.

Enticements

There is a great store in Los Angeles called Trader Joe's. It is a gourmet food store, offering an unending variety of products and foods from around the world. However, from time to time they also offer limited quantities of something special. One day they will have twenty cases of Chilean wine for $4 per bottle. Another day they will offer a crate filled with one-pound lots of Belgian chocolate. Customers know they can get gourmet foods at Trader Joe's, but they also know there is always some special little treat hidden in the aisles waiting for them. All they have to do is go in, and yes, the parking lot is filled almost every hour of the day.

For a Web site, the use of sweepstakes, Easter eggs, and special offers all help to do the same thing. They create an expectation for the consumer that a special prize awaits them inside the site. The more often this can be repeated, the better. If, like in the Trader Joe's example, a con-

---

[29] One of the best books on the value of building an online community is *Net Gain* by John Hagle III and Arthur G. Armstrong, Harvard Business School Press, 1997.

sumer knows there is some hidden prize waiting on the right Web page, they have an incentive to return often. Just make sure whatever promotion is being run delivers on the consumer's expectation. For some sites, having the most up-to-date news is enough. For others, creating prize elements is needed.

Regardless of what you do, make sure it is consistent and make sure people are never disappointed. Nothing is worse than letting someone down on his or her expectations.

Sweepstakes

Sweepstakes can be an incredible tool to do more than just drive traffic. Not only do they provide incentive for online customers to visit a particular URL, they enable the Web site to collect demographic information on those entering and create sponsorship opportunities for the site to sell.[30]

As an introductory event, a sweepstakes is an excellent way to encourage first-time users. By promoting the sweepstakes as well as your site, you will encourage those people at first reticent to enter with a reason to enter and provide information.

There are three important components of any sweepstakes—the prize, the association to the site, and the questions for the entrants. Simply put, the larger the prize, the more people will visit your site and enter and the more partners you can attract. After the prize, the more association the sweepstakes has to the site, the more memorable it will be. For instance, if a flower site gave away $100, it would drive traffic. However, giving away $100 worth of flowers on Valentine's Day will probably make more people remember the site. Rather than just creating an opportunity to win something, you need to give people a reason to remember it. Finally, the fewer elements a sweepstakes requires for entry, the more people will enter.

Theme

The easiest way to find a theme for your sweepstakes is to look at a calendar. There are plenty of events to tie into—graduation day, Father's Day, Mother's Day, Easter, and the summer solstice—are all great ways to target a different market niche or product category. Best of all, if a particular holiday doesn't work for you, create your own. It's the beauty of

---

[30] For more information on setting up a sponsorship, see chapter 5—Preparing Your Site to Profit.

a sweepstakes. As long as you are the one giving something away, you can call the shots.

Prizes

Once you create a theme for the sponsorship, you will need to create a prize package. If you have travel for a theme, the prize package could be a weekend getaway. If you sell flowers, the prize package could be a dozen roses. If you are providing sports news, the prize can be a set of golf clubs or a pair of season tickets. The million-dollar question is where to find the prizes and who is going to pay for them. Most Web sites have three choices for this: first, pay for them yourself; second, trade for them; and third, sell sponsorships to advertisers.

For obvious reasons, I will pass over paying for prizes. If you have the money, getting a prize is just a matter of how much you are willing to spend. If not, you will be trading the promotional value of your Web site and the sweepstakes for prizes. If you can guarantee a certain level of traffic or the ability to deliver a targeted audience, you can sell a sponsorship. If not, you will have to give away logo placement in exchange for prizes.[31]

If this is your first sweepstakes, put your time into getting prizes, not paid sponsors. This is not as bad as it sounds. With a prize you will be getting traffic, and after a successful sweepstakes, you will have a story to tell advertisers when you are trying to sell a sponsorship.

Design

The sweepstakes itself is a very easy component to design. It should consist of a primary page that links to your site, a rules page, a prize description page, and a response page. Although each of these pages is primarily there to provide the visitor with price information or legal information, it does not have to be boring. Add as many graphics as you can to this without burdening it. Make it memorable, and don't forget to add promotional text to drive people back to your site.

Primary Page   The primary page should include a description of the sweepstakes, the prizes being offered, and the entry form. Depending on the information you are trying to capture from entrants, the entry form

---

[31] Until you have run several sweepstakes and can provide a story or case study to potential advertisers, do not even try to sell sponsorships. Advertisers will want proof their advertising dollars are being spent well, and the proof comes from the result of past sweepstakes.

should at least capture the entrant's name, email address, and mailing address. This will enable you to contact the entrant should they win. Any information captured beyond that is a bonus and will help you create a profile of your user (e.g., age, gender, education, income).

Once the entrant enters their information and clicks on an entry button, the data should feed into a database and be maintained until the sweepstakes has ended. The resulting database can be as simple as an Excel file, or as complex as you want.

Rules Page   Linked to the primary page should be a rules page.[32] The only objective of this page is to protect yourself from lawsuits. It does not have to be pretty, just thorough. Rules vary greatly between county, state, and country, and protecting yourself today means getting a lawyer involved.

Product Description Page   This an optional page, to provide entrants a full description of the prizes being offered. Although it is used to draw people in, it is also used to protect the Web site by leaving nothing to the imagination of the entrant and providing a complete description of the prizes offered. Depending on the prize itself, the information on the primary page is often enough.

Selecting Winners

For some sweepstakes using a random number generation program is enough to select the winner. Other sweepstakes may require the use of an independent organization to select a winner. Whichever way your lawyers tell you to go, remember the selection of a winner must be left completely to chance. This means no talent or ability can come into play. Once you begin selecting winners by their ability to write a better poem or get high score on a game, it is no longer left to chance, and subject to different rules. Again, contact a lawyer before proceeding.

Easter Eggs

On the Internet, a hidden prize is referred to as an Easter egg. The prizes can be free products or discount offers. Typically, a line of code is inserted into a page that refers to a random number generator. When a specific page is accessed, the program sends a message to show a specific icon. For instance, every time a page downloads one hundred times, a small

---

[32] See appendix 7 for a sample rules page.

button will appear within the text that tells the reader they have won. This message can be in the shape of a gold coin, an egg, or any other image that, when found and clicked, sends the winner to an entry page. Winners can then enter their email address and prizes can be awarded via email.

The benefit of an Easter egg is its ability to drive traffic. Because they appear at random times and on random pages, consumers have to look for them by clicking on multiple pages, increasing page impression levels. Because there are multiple winners, prizes for Easter eggs do not have to be as expensive to entice winners. They can include product discounts, coupons, or even samples.

As with any online promotion, the greater the value, the more traffic it will drive, and, as with sweepstakes, it is advisable to consult a lawyer to determine what rules must be followed and what legalities apply to your area and to your Web site.

OTD/OTW—Of The Day/Of The Week

An excellent tool to drive traffic and bring people back to a Web site is to create an OTD or OTW. Commonly, these include daily or weekly pictures, horoscopes or stories, but they can include almost any information that changes on a daily basis.

The Web site Bikini.com has a very effective pic of the day that has become one of the more highly trafficked areas on the Web site. Latimes.com has a site recommendation area that suggests new sites with relevance to a news story or other calendar event. Both of these are created to bring consumers back to the sites in search of new content.

As with anything on the Internet, the most important element is finding something consumers will be willing to return to. A picture of a beautiful woman seems to have an amazing ability to attract traffic to a male-oriented site. A daily recipe has the ability to drive traffic to a cooking site. However, make sure what you do is consistent and provides the consumer with something they will not be disappointed to receive.

As its name implies, an OTD needs new content on a daily basis and an OTW requires weekly content. If you are not sure how much work is required, start off with fresh weekly content with plans to go daily if you find success. Better still, create a way for readers to enter their own pictures, quotes, or stories. Not only does this provide content, it will drive even more traffic from people trying to see if their submission was selected. Whichever way you decide to go, the traffic daily content can drive will almost always offset the work required to deliver it.

Slideshows

If you are looking for a way to increase the number of page impressions your Web site receives, a slideshow may be the answer. A slideshow is a program that automatically refreshes a Web page, sending the customer a new image or new information automatically. Just like a traditional slideshow, an online slideshow allows the viewer to just sit back and watch the images change. Because the customer does not have to continually click to access a new page, slideshows can deliver a new image every few seconds increasing the number of page impressions a customer will normally access.

Further, because a slideshow is automatic, once it is created, it requires little if any intervention from the Web developer.

Linking

Online consumers rely on links to find Web sites of interest. These can include hypertext links from stories and content to awards or icons and logos. Regardless of its form, nonadvertising links created between sites are one of the most useful elements to driving traffic. The reason is simple: They provide a way for the consumer to access additional information that is relevant to them. As always their ability to provide *relevant* information is the key to their success. There are two types of links, one-way links and two-way links. One-way links provide a link to your site; two-way links provide reciprocal links to and from a Web site. As you may imagine, the second type is much easier to create since both parties benefit.

Regardless of how you decide to create your links program, try to develop a series of buttons or logos in various sizes. This not only provides an easy way for other sites to include your link, but it establishes your site and maintains your brand. If you are able to create links from a number of sites in a particular category, you will be able to position yourself as a resource to consumers.

For instance, if someone is looking for a surfboard on the Internet and repeatedly sees your logo on various surfing sites, there is an implied authority attached to it. Similar to traditional advertising, repeating an ad causes the consumer to make an association with your logo that lasts far longer than a click.

Links Page

At one point, creating a link required nothing more than asking another Web site to link to yours. Now, with design and space at a premium, many sites are reluctant to do so and require a reciprocal link from your site to theirs. This becomes tricky. You want to have other sites drive traffic to you, but you don't want to lose traffic to a better site. To avoid this, locate sites that are good, but not better than yours, or that focus on complementary and noncompetitive categories. This could include vendors, suppliers, or providers of ancillary information.

A good way to create a reciprocal linking program is to simply create a resources or link page. This provides you with a way to provide orderly links to other sites without having to place them in key content areas.

Awards Programs

A second way to create a link is to develop an award program. An award is simply a logo that can be placed on another Web site creating a link back to your home page. The award can be attached to an email and sent to appropriate sites.

However, similar to the links page, it may be smart to create an awards page, because many sites will request a reciprocal link back to their site.

INTEGRATING THE ELEMENTS INTO AN ONLINE CAMPAIGN

Like any advertising campaign, an online campaign is a direct result of budget. The more money you have available, the more you will be able to promote your business. However, because there is a surplus of advertising inventory on the Internet, a very effective online ad campaign can be maintained on a very small or even no budget. The only difference is the amount of negotiating you will need to conduct and the amount of real estate on your Web site you will have to give up.

Regardless of your budget, focus on incorporating as much off-site content into your campaign as possible. The idea behind using content to drive traffic means creating a series of "teasers" that are located on other sites. Such co-branded areas, micro-sites, or sponsorships not only leverage your existing content, but give the consumer a hint of what lies beyond their click. For a Web site this expands the site's effectiveness beyond its URL; for non-sites this drives the product to where the customer is, rather than attempting to draw the customer to the product. Under both circumstances this greatly increases your ability to qualify your customer before they click because they have a better idea of what waits for them beyond the click.

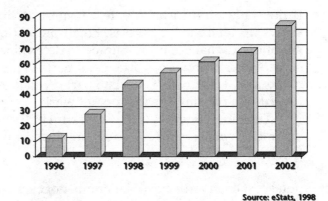

Source: eStats, 1998

U.S. Net User Growth, in Millions

Benchmarking and Goal Setting

The first step in creating an online campaign is developing a goal and creating some benchmarks for success. The easiest goal is the amount of traffic you want on your site. Based on growth projections, the average increase in Internet traffic is somewhere between 30 percent and 40 percent per year. This means your site should increase by this amount with a minimum of advertising just by riding the wave of overall online traffic.

With a minimum of advertising, you should be able to double the size of your site's traffic every year. This means maintaining a monthly growth rate of 7 percent. If you have a substantial budget, you should be able to increase this growth in proportion to the money you intend to spend. The most important part of benchmarking where you are and creating a goal for your advertising is being realistic. During June, July, and August you will notice slower growth due to universities and colleges going on summer vacation.[33] In December you will notice a drop during the last two weeks. This is nothing to be shocked with, it just means driving more traffic during the off-summer months.

Tracking Advertising

The second part of any campaign is tracking success. One of the greatest benefits of online advertising is the ability to track everything you do.

---

[33] Most universities and colleges offer free Internet access to students. When the students leave for vacation, they lose their free access and overall Internet traffic usually faces a significant drop.

Banner ads produce click rates. Hypertext links produce traffic that shows up on basic log reports. Email promotions can drive traffic to a specific URL that can be monitored to determine exactly how many consumers visited and when. The good part is you will quickly know what works and what doesn't. The bad part is you don't have as many excuses to continue running ads that do not work.

The most common way to measure traffic from a banner campaign or content sponsorship is to measure the cost per click. This is a simple formula:

Total cost of advertising/Total number of clicks received = Cost per click

This formula allows you to measure exactly how much you are paying for each click regardless of how it is being delivered and the manner of the advertising.

For other advertising models, such as sponsorships or micro-sites that have multiple links, log files allow you to track exactly where your traffic is coming from. A common program is called Web Trends. Web Trends provides such information as total hits, page views, unique users, and referring URLs and Web sites, in addition to much more. However, these numbers will allow you to find and track exactly where your traffic is coming from.

Regardless of which method you use, it is important to track each element. Those that do not work should be replaced by elements that provide results. However, as you will see, producing clicks is not the only goal of a campaign and is not the only way to measure its success.

Combining Tools to Create a Campaign

There are two components to every campaign—brand and tactical advertising. As its name implies, the primary objective of brand advertising is used to increase brand awareness. Tactical advertising, on the other hand, is used to drive traffic or produce bottom-line results. The goal of an effective advertising campaign is to create advertising that both builds a brand and produces results.

For this reason it is important to combine several elements into one campaign. Banner advertising alone may only produce a 1 percent or 2 percent click-through, but when combined with a sponsored content area, this click rate will most likely double. The reason for this is simple. The various advertising messages reinforce each other and are thus more effective in both building awareness and driving traffic.

As you can see, and as I have established throughout this book, maintaining a consistent campaign that promotes one look, one feel, and one brand is essential to the consumer being able to instantly recognize the advertising and more readily respond to it.

Building a Campaign

Step 1—Public Relations

After posting your site with search engines, the first step to promoting a new Web presence or a change in content is by issuing a press release. This should be done as the new area is launched to try to capitalize on any press-worthy attention the new content can generate.

Step 2—Promotions and Sweepstakes

Creating a sweepstakes or other promotional tool at the launch of a site or the start of an advertising campaign is one of the best ways to drive traffic. It will have to be promoted, but it provides a reason for consumers to visit. Even if they do not know your product, they will respond to the chance to win. Using a sweepstakes or promotion as a basis for a campaign will increase the click rate of your advertising. Although these clicks will also come from consumers just looking to enter the sweepstakes, it will drive borderline consumers who may not normally visit.

Step 3—Banner Trades

Depending on your resources, the first part of any campaign should be developing banner trades with noncompeting Web sites. Unless you have a very large budget, I would not recommend buying banners as a way to promote your Web site. They simply will not produce the kind of return you want to create a jump in traffic. Instead, begin by trading your impression inventory with theirs. Although I am not a big fan of banner advertising, it is the easiest and quickest way to begin expanding your online presence.

If you do not have enough inventory to effect a trade or you have money to spend on banners, only purchase banners on smaller targeted sites. The cost per click will probably be lower than on larger, more expensive sites. Try to effect a $.10 to $.20 cost per click. On smaller sites this is possible, but larger sites will probably cost around $.50 per click. If you are paying anything more than $.50, take your advertising elsewhere.

Step 4—Offsite Content Development

If you want to see an immediate jump in traffic, begin to negotiate co-branded content areas. These are the teasers that will go on other sites with multiple links back to yours. Although these usually require a bit more work designing and compiling the content, the multiple links they carry and their ability to attract an audience on an ongoing basis makes them much more effective as an advertising tool.

These can include creating a sponsored content area, developing a co-branded area on another site, or trading content.

Step 5—Banner Buys

Only after you have begun to develop offsite content should you begin buying banner advertisements. The reason for this is simple. Banner ads will produce some level of response and they will help build brand awareness; however, their effectiveness increases dramatically depending on the content they are run against. Coordinating a banner buy with sponsored content creates an effective use of advertising dollars. Running banners on their own usually will not produce the results you want.

Step 6—Offline Advertising

Unless you have an ample advertising budget, an offline campaign should be implemented only after your online efforts have produced results. Offline advertising is expensive. It produces a lower response from its audience simply because that audience is not on the Internet. Running advertising on the Internet allows you to test which online consumers respond and then craft any offline advertising to target those users.

Campaign Calendar

One of the easiest ways to ensure an online advertising campaign remains on track is to create a campaign calendar. This is simply a way to maintain a coordinated advertising effort and ensure your efforts work together effectively.

A sample of a calendar follows. You will notice each line indicates a separate site and a separate buy or trade. Additionally, the paid online advertising is halted during summer but resumed in September to avoid buying advertising during the summer vacation at colleges and universities. In addition, this advertising is bought in alternating months. The reason for this is to ensure advertising stays fresh and maintains a high click rate. Since it is paid for, extra attention should be paid to retaining the highest ROI possible.

Component	Jan	Feb	Mar	Apr	May	Jun	Jul	Aug	Sep	Oct
Site Launch										
Press Release		2/15								
Sweepstakes		2/15-3/15								
Banner Trades										
Site X		start 2/1 250,000/mos.								
Site Y		start 2/1 250,000/mos.								
Site Z		start 2/1 100,000/mos.								
Banner Buy										
Site M (100K @$15cpm)										
Site M (200K @$8cpm)										
Site M (50K @$25cpm)										
Content Sponsorship										
Site A										
Site B										

Marketing Calendar

CONCLUSION

Like any product, the ability to market and promote a Web site is reliant on one feature—that Web site's ability to deliver. If it does not have the content or the information the consumer is looking for, they may visit once, but they will never return. The art of effective marketing is knowing what you have, and being able to find the customers who are interested in it. The rest lies in crafting a message to which your customers will respond.

Simply put, do not try to market something you don't have or are not. It will only waste your time and that of your customers.

CHAPTER FIVE

Preparing Your Site to Profit

It's why we're here: profit. Some want to sell products via ecommerce. Some want to sell advertising. For those who just want to create a presence to build a brand, you may still want to read this section. If you think selling advertising takes away from the value of the site, just take a look at what Intuit is doing on its small business section, or what VISA is doing on Rankit.com. Each has incorporated advertising and sponsorships into its business model. And from the advertisers they have attracted, each is doing a very good job at it.

Profiting on the Net does not mean breaking up your site into content packages and selling it at the loss of your brand. It means creating an opportunity for advertisers to speak with their customers in an ad-friendly environment. You guessed it; it means creating content that responds to the needs of advertisers, or identifying advertisers that will want the audience you are already attracting.

There are three primary ways to generate revenue from an online presence: selling advertising, selling products through ecommerce, or charging a subscription fee. The majority of this chapter focuses on selling advertising. I do this for one reason. A site that generates income from ecommerce will probably not want to direct someone's attention to another Web site and another buying opportunity. The goal of an ecommerce site is to capture its customers' attention and drive them to a purchase opportunity using content. The creation of branded content the customer responds to has already been covered. At this point, the only components missing are ecommerce and fulfillment mechanisms. Both are technical components of a Web site and any recommendation a print book could make would be outdated by the time it was printed.

Similarly, a subscription-based online presence will want to retain a clean design that does not interfere with its customer's experience. Interference makes for unhappy customers and fewer subscriptions. Again, the creation of branded content a customer responds to is essential to creating a reliable customer base. At this point, the only thing missing is the billing mechanism; and again, this is a technical element for which any recommendation would be hopelessly outdated by the time this book was printed.

In both instances, I will make note of key elements that have been shown to lead to successful ecommerce and subscription business models. In addition, this book will present the reader with resources that will present them with the latest technologies to allow them to choose.

SELLING ADVERTISING

Jupiter Communications estimates that 26 percent of the top 100 and 42 percent of the top 50 Web publishers host sponsored areas now. In addition, by 2001, Jupiter estimates 50 percent of all online ad dollars will go toward co-branded content rather than to banner ads.

This does not mean the banner ad is going away. It does mean to sell advertising you must look beyond simply selling banner ads. Advertisers are looking to do more than just buy 100,000 banner ad impressions at a 1 percent click-through rate. They want to find opportunities in which they can leverage the value of the online content. To accommodate the advertisers, Web sites must create opportunities for sponsorship of content areas.

The best approach I have found to selling online advertising is to sell banner impressions in order to create short-term revenue, and to sell sponsorship packages for longer-term revenue. This dual approach works for two reasons. First, selling banner advertising takes much less time than selling sponsorships, so it can be turned over quickly to produce more immediate revenue. However, banner advertising will produce smaller revenues due to the lower levels of spending on banner campaigns. So, for long-term success sponsorship advertising must be offered.

Banner Advertising

Types

There are three basic types of banner ads currently being sold—static, animated, and interactive. Already static banners are a thing of the past. They produce low results because they are less visible to the user, and as technology progresses animated and interactive banners will continue to become more prominent.

As its name implies a static banner displays a message that does not change. As expected, because nothing stands out to attract the eye of the consumer, they produce very low click-through rates and perform poorly in branding exercises. At this point in time there is little reason to create or use a static banner ad.

An improvement over static banners is the animated banner ad. These simply contain some form of movement in the banner space. This movement has proven to be more effective at drawing attention and increasing click-through rates.

Interactive banners allow online consumers to interact with them. This interaction includes small games that consumers can play or poses questions to the user, helping the advertiser to pre-qualify users based on their needs.

To effectively price banner advertising, first assess what your competition is selling their ads for. Most publishers list ad rates on their sites. For those who don't it is an easy process to telephone or email them and ask.

Specifications

Regardless of what type of banner ad is used, the Interactive Advertising Bureau has established a standard for banner advertisements. Banners are sized by the number of pixels in each (i.e., 468 $\times$ 60 pixels). Most Web sites will set a limit (usually 10K) for the size of each, regardless of the graphic image sizes. Standard sizes are:[34]

- Full banner—468 $\times$ 60 pixels
- Half banner—234 $\times$ 60 pixels
- Vertical banner—120 $\times$ 240 pixels
- Button 1—120 $\times$ 90 pixels
- Button 2—120 $\times$ 60 pixels
- Square button—125 $\times$ 125 pixels
- Micro button—88 $\times$ 31 pixels

When selling banner advertisements a space on your Web site must be created that can accommodate the placement of the standard banner ad (i.e., 468 $\times$ 60).

---

[34] The Internet Advertising Bureau Web site has a complete listing of all banner sizes with applicable images. It is located at *www.iab.net*.

Selling Banner Ads

First, companies buying banners are going for a return on their investment. This is measured by click-through rates or through cost per acquisition. Either way, advertisers want proof of how much traffic is driven to their site. Further, although banner ads may draw attention, they have yet to produce the emotional reaction a television commercial can. So as long as advertisers are using them to produce a return, don't try to sell them on the branding benefits. That is not what they will want. Instead sell them to drive traffic. For companies who want to brand, think in terms of beyond-the-banner opportunities.

Content-Based Advertising

According to the Internet Advertising Bureau, revenues from sponsorships continue to grow steadily. It estimates 1997 Q3 sponsorship revenues to be $93 million, representing 41 percent of total online ad revenue.

Noticing their effectiveness in both branding and driving traffic, many advertisers are looking to move beyond the banner. They want to take a greater part in the content itself, and share in the reader's attention to that content.

Examples of content-based advertising include:

Sponsored Content

Sponsorships are very similar to event-style sponsorships. These primarily include logo placement, but can incorporate some form of sweepstakes, content creation, couponing, or product sampling. Content advertising is appealing because it:

- Creates a long-term relationship with the advertiser that can grow.
- Enables the publisher to sell larger advertising packages.
- Reacts to the advertiser's need for more integrated advertising programs.
- Appeals to advertisers who want a larger, broader ad presence.
- Assists you in building your site.

The key to success in selling content advertising is to not sell it. Unlike the banner, advertisers quickly know which content is appropriate

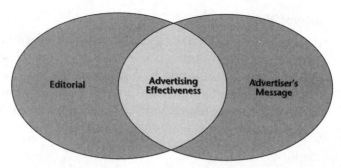

Creating Targeted Opportunities for Niche Advertisers

for them and which is not. It is more efficient to see what advertisers are currently doing, assess how they regard their brand, and match them with specific content areas based on that match. Save yourself the time and your advertisers the frustration of trying to sell what they don't need or want. Work instead on connecting them to the right content.

Advertorials

Advertorials differ from sponsorships depending on who retains editorial control. In the sponsorship model, the publisher has control. In the advertorial model, the advertiser has control and the content is usually not labeled as sponsored content. This makes it difficult for the consumer to discern which content is advertising and which is editorial. Because of this, the consumer often feels misled by the content and the publisher, leading to a backlash against the advertiser and the publisher.

For a publisher, once the editorial integrity of their content has been compromised, the value of that advertising on that content decreases (think the *New York Times* vs. *National Enquirer*), so think twice before selling your one asset—the value of your content—by labeling it clearly.

Product Placement

Product placement, as its name implies, is the actual placement of product into the editorial context of the site. As long as the content is appropriate and the product is well defined, product placement works very well. The most common way to do this is to create a sweepstakes or other promotion in which the product itself is integral to the content. Like the advertorial, beware of product placement in a situation where the consumer might feel misled (e.g., product reviews).

Interstitials

Interstitials have been called advertisus interuptus by too many people to ignore the term. Interstitials are full or partial-screen advertisements that pop up, dominating and interrupting the consumer's experience. They are considered intrusive and a nuisance by consumers. For this reason, many advertiser and publishers steer clear of them.

Successful Selling

Don't Sell, Connect

Nobody wants to pick up the phone and hear, "Hey, have I got a deal for you." Almost any media buyer has been burned enough times to not listen any further. Regardless of whether they work directly for a company or for an agency, media buyers want three things: First, an opportunity that brings their products to their customers; second, a complete advertising package which will not require more work for them; and third, a problem-free experience in which the advertising bought is delivered as promised with full reporting.

Because of this, the last thing any salesperson wants to do is sell. Instead, the salesperson needs to first find out what the advertiser is looking for and then provide them with the facts that prove why their's is the right place to be.

Target Advertiser's Audiences

The first rule of selling advertising is to only go after the advertisers who are trying to reach your audience. As simple as this sounds, you would be surprised at how many media buyers and marketing managers are contacted by Web sites that simply target the wrong audience.

Advertisers know who their audience is. They know who is buying their product. Save yourself the time and energy it takes to track down an advertiser and first create a list of products that have a direct connection to your site. If your site targets preteens, it will only waste your time to pursue an automobile manufacturer no matter how much they are spending. Preteens do not buy cars.

To Sell or to Educate

The second rule is actually more of a choice. You can either spend your time selling or spend your time educating. Rather than approach advertisers who are not actively buying online advertising, first identify those who are already aware of the benefits of online advertising. Why spend months teaching a marketing manager the benefits of online advertising? Why not spend your time going after advertisers who are already spending ad dollars online?

Bring in Brands

Advertisers are more comfortable placing their ads on a site that is running brand name advertising. If your Web site is currently running advertisements for a local sports store, a brand like Coca-Cola will be less likely to look at you as a national player. Before you actively sell advertising, try to attract as large a brand as you can, even if it means giving some page impressions away for free. If an advertiser sees Coca-Cola, Volkswagen, and Ray Ban running advertising on your site, it's a better indication of your ability to deliver an audience than if they see Bob's Tackle Shop, EZ Credit, or Betty's Hot Babes.

Lower Your Expectations—At First

The price of online banner advertising has been dropping almost since it began. The reason for this is simple. There is too much inventory and not enough demand. Almost every site wants to reach a $25 CPM, however, few achieve it. Advertisers realize they can purchase banner advertising for between $6 and $20 CPM on sites that will deliver qualified traffic (see Buying Advertising on Top 100 Sites).

When you first start advertising, lower your prices to attract better name advertisers. Your goal at first is to create a story. If an advertiser paying a $5 CPM receives a 6 percent click-through rate, that is something you can tell to another advertiser. If an advertiser paying a $5 CPM is able to attract 1,500 new customers, that is something you can tell to another advertiser. Once you have a story, you can raise your prices, but in order to have that story you need to bring in your first advertiser. The easiest way to do that is through lower pricing.

Offer Incentives

Very few online advertisers will purchase a banner campaign without knowing what to expect. If you have excess inventory, offer a prospective advertiser a limited run for low or no ad dollars to get them to try your site. If you offer an advertiser a no-risk offer, it becomes very hard for them to turn it down. However, just make sure they will be willing to buy if the test is successful.

When you offer a test, add a simple clause that guarantees they will purchase advertising if the test meets certain criteria. There are several ways to do this. For instance:

- If site X runs a 100,000 impression test campaign for an advertiser, and that campaign produces better than a 1 percent return, that advertiser agrees to pay for the test at a $5 CPM. If it fails to produce above a 1 percent return, the advertising is free.
- If site X runs a 100,000 impression test campaign for an advertiser, and that campaign produces more than 100 new sign-ups, the advertiser agrees to run an additional 1,000,000 impressions at a rate of $10 CPM.

Preparing Your Site and Yourself for Advertising

Know Your Customer

The first question any advertiser will ask you is who is your reader. If you don't know this, don't even try to sell. There are several ways to find this out. First, look into your log files. Every time a Web page is delivered to a reader, it creates a file that includes basic user information such as the file's name, time it was delivered, and address where it was delivered. Based on this information, a Webmaster can generate a report that will tell the country of origin, the domain name, and the Web page that user entered from. This will help you create a basic outline of who your reader is.

In addition, time spent on a site, entrance and exit pages, and the number of visits can be ascertained. The longer time a person spends on your page the better. The better quality of sites your reader visits from, the better.

Another way to create a picture of your user is to create a sweepstakes. By offering a prize of varying levels, the publisher can find out basic demographic information of the user. Key information to ask is age, gender, income, and zip code.

Verify Your Traffic

If you can, hire a company to add credibility to your reports. This involves hiring a company to perform an audit of your Web pages. This will generate a report for a specific time period that verifies your traffic. If you cannot afford an audit, consider hiring an ad server company such as NetGravity that audits its ad delivery.

Create Serving/Reporting

Every advertiser will want reports from you. These reports will be daily or weekly and will include impressions delivered, click-throughs delivered, and click-through rates for each ad. Advertisers and agencies will want these reports on a weekly basis at a minimum, so you have to be prepared to deliver them.

These reports are integrated into almost every ad serving technology. The best way to start is to use a basic ad serving program until you have paying advertisers. This usually includes a line of code that pulls a banner ad from a specific file. When you begin to attract paid advertisers, invest in an ad system based on a cost per ad delivered, such as Doubleclick's Dart program. With this system, you will be able to deliver ads without having to pay for expensive software to run it. As your ad sales increase, increase your ad delivery system incrementally. The key is low risk, high return.

Build Ad Packages

It is easier to go to an advertiser with a series of advertising packages for them to choose from. Although they will probably not buy a package outright, it will enable them to see what kind of advertising you are selling. Most media buyers have very little time, and hate nothing more than to spend 30 minutes talking to someone in general terms without having a concrete program to start from.

Your site should already be created with vertical segments. Each of these segments will probably attract a specific advertiser. By creating advertising packages that combine banner advertising, sponsored content, advertorials, sweepstakes, you can produce a robust package advertisers want. Show that you are willing to work with the advertiser to meet their needs by creating robust packages that can be altered to meet advertiser's goals and objectives while fitting into their budgets.[35]

A good combination for an advertising package would include general banner advertising opportunities, a sweepstakes opportunity, and a sponsorship opportunity. Creating one package for each section of the site means you can approach an advertiser with an opportunity tailored to meet their needs. Ideally, such an opportunity would be complete enough to only require a sign-off to implement it. The more guesswork involved, the more opportunity the advertiser has to turn it down.

---

[35] An outline for a sample ad package is included in appendix 8.

Consider a Rep Firm or Network

In the beginning, unless you are already a well-known brand or have the resources to sell yourself, consider hiring an advertising rep firm or joining a network. Selling advertising is a full-time job. It means making cold calls to companies and agencies. It means writing, printing, and mailing advertising packages. It means following up on sales calls with more calls and revised proposals. It takes a lot of work, and it is very easy to let it fall through the cracks.

The payoff for doing this is you will know what advertisers want firsthand, and you will be able to talk about your site better and with more enthusiasm than any outside salesperson can do. It also means you will not have to pay an outside firm for selling your site.

The alternative is hiring a rep firm. They will typically charge between 30 percent to 50 percent commission, and will demand a retainer and one-year contract. However, they will generally be able to move your inventory quickly, and will free you up to manage your site and sell higher-priced sponsorships. Before you go with a rep firm, first determine if you want their advertisers running on your site. Second, see what other Web sites they represent. Make sure you will be in good company—a bad banner can ruin an entire Web page.

Another option is to join an ad network. You will most likely pay between 20 percent to 50 percent in commissions, but there is usually no retainer to worry about. Depending on the content of your site, there are a number of networks that may be appropriate. Such networks as Flycast, DoubleClick, and Adsmart have different strengths and weaknesses. Similar to the rep firms, assess what kind of advertisers they work with, and whose company you will share before joining.

Finally, when dealing with any rep firm, make sure you have an out. Guarantee yourself that if they do not present your site in the manner you want it presented, you can withdraw from the contract. Additionally, guarantee yourself that you will be able to sell a certain amount of advertisements yourself. Many rep firms demand to be the only one selling your advertising. Although this sounds like an easy way out at first, you will quickly find yourself losing income when an advertiser calls you directly.

Finding Your Advertisers

Use Your Competition to Find Your Advertisers

One of the best ways to find an active online advertiser who is targeting your audience or your product is through your competition. Simply visit other Web sites and see what advertisers are running on their site. If you want to contact one of the advertisers, follow the ad back to their site, then use the InterNIC (located at *www.internic.com*) and the advertiser's Web site URL to find the phone number and address of the advertiser through the InterNIC's search process. The rest takes a phone call and persistence.

Before you call, find out how they are spending their money and see what their goals are by looking at their offers and the kind of ad they are running. Again, the easiest way to bring an online advertiser to your site is to offer them a test or other incentive to try your site over your competition.

The Red Book

Long a staple of ad salespeople, the *Red Book* is an annual guide to finding company executives. Although it is somewhat expensive (approximately $1,000), it is the best way to find out who to contact. Companies are listed by name, SIC code, and geography. If you do not have one, or cannot afford one, try your local library.

The *Red Book* also lists the advertising agencies of most companies along with specific contact information. I have found it is best to call the advertiser directly. Have them refer you to their agency. Approaching the advertiser first provides you with an opportunity to sell directly. More likely, it will provide you with an introduction to the agency, giving you a bit more leverage with the agency itself.

Agency Lists

There are numerous Web sites that list specific advertising agencies. Channel Seven, located at *www.channelseven.com*, contains a list of the larger interactive agencies. The American Association of Advertising Agencies, located at *www.aaaa.com*, is another source for agency information.

At this time, it is probably more efficient to focus only on interactive agencies. Most of the larger agencies have already created smaller new media units. My experience has been that most traditional agencies that do not have an online unit rarely deal with online advertising dollars. As with advertisers, find out the client lists of agencies before you contact them. Most online agencies have a Web site that lists their clients. When you do contact them, ask for the account director or media director for a specific client.

Remember, your goal is not to try to sell your site, rather it is to show the agency the benefits of your site, and how those apply to their clients. Every account team has a set of goals and criteria with which it buys online advertising. Your job is to find out what they are looking for and see if your Web site can deliver. If it cannot, you will only waste your time trying to sell a product that does not fit into the media plan.

ECOMMERCE

Ecommerce is a wide-ranging category that includes sales of everything from computers to fish. In addition, there are standard catalog sales, auctions, and more. If you can think of a way to sell it offline, there's a way to do the same thing online. As you will find from almost any on-line ecommerce site, the actual sales mechanism used is less a factor in closing a sale as the consumer's shopping experience. Face it—as long as the cash register works quickly and efficiently that's not what closes a sale. It's the salesperson and the product that sells. So, if you are un-familiar with ecommerce programs, do your research or hire a consul-tant as most of the successful online retailers have done. Do what you do best and sell. Leave the cash registers to someone who knows how to run them.

Creating a Sales Experience

While researching this book, one of the most consistent responses I re-ceived from successful ecommerce sites was not about their technology; it was about the lack of it. The most successful sites are those that make

- Convenience:
  - Well laid-out site/easy navigation
  - All necessary product, sales and policy information is available and accessible.
  - Checkout/payment process is fast and all final costs are clearly identified.
- Security:
  - Credit card transaction must be (or be perceived to be) secure.
  - The use of personal information is clearly spelled out.
  - Merchant identity in "real-space" is disclosed and highlighted.
- Customer Services:
  - Access to customer service representatives is easy and timely.
  - Multiple access methods are available (email, toll-free phone, fax).
  - Return, warranty and service policies are spelled-out upfront.
- Variety:
  - Wide variety of products and services offered within the site.
- Price:
  - Competitive pricing.

Source: eStats, 1998

Top Five Factors for Turning Online Shoppers into Buyers

the shopping experience easy and fun and that mirror the offline shopping experience. FultonStreet.com, an online fish market, credits their success to treating the customer special; Bluefly.com has created a personal shopper to enhance its customer relationships. Both of these Web sites hired outside companies to manage the sales mechanisms, leaving them to do what they do best—sell.[36]

Bluefly.com recognized early on that the many shoppers treated their shopping experience like content. For many, shopping is a form of entertainment. In response, they created a sales experience that acted like a personal shopper to the customer. This is a highly personalized service that makes recommendations based on each customer's profile. Not only does this provide them with hours of entertainment, it also drives them to a purchase mechanism.

As you will see in the Bluefly case study, creating a shopping experience the customer is comfortable with is essential to creating an online shopping experience that works. Content is what drives people to make a purchase, but as Bluefly.com noted, having a cash register that works is essential to closing the sale.

A Short Path to Purchase

Online consumers do not want to wind their way through a maze to find information. Why would they want to do the same thing to make a purchase? They don't and they won't.

Whatever search engine or catalog software you use, make sure the customer is at most two clicks away from making a purchase. The longer it takes for the customer to reach the cash register, the more likely they are to leave. Why give them the opportunity?

The Barnes & Noble Express Cart is an excellent example of this. While other sites rely on shopping cart technology, Barnes & Noble created a way for one-book purchasers to go directly to the checkout counter. Granted, shopping carts are currently one of the best technologies to allow multiple purchases while a consumer browses, but they necessitate at least two additional steps on most sites. This means two additional ways for the consumer to reconsider buying—and that is two too many.

In addition, once the customer has reached the checkout counter, all they should need to do is enter their information and click a button. Do not worry about up-selling them until after they have checked out.

---

[36] Case studies for both Bluefly and FultonStreet can be found in chapter 7.

Trying to sell too much prior to their entering a credit card number and clicking OK, risks sending them off to another site.

High Quality vs. Low Prices

Aside from entertainment, consumers shop on the Internet for two primary reasons—ease of use and lower prices. Although some Web sites offer low-priced goods for even less, this is probably not the best tactic for one reason. It is easy enough for consumers to purchase low-priced products offline. Additionally, unless they are buying in bulk, any savings they receive online is quickly lost in shipping charges. Small savings and the need to wait for delivery does not make this a very appealing prospect.

What is appealing to most customers is a true bargain—high quality at low prices. FultonStreet.com sells exceedingly high quality products at a discount. Bluefly.com sells designer fashions for less than outlet stores. They take the savings inherent in running an online business (e.g., not having a brick and mortar store) and pass it on to the consumer.

Consumers have two primary reasons for not shopping online—anticipation of a long delivery time and the risk of not receiving what they ordered. To overcome these barriers, the promised benefits have to outweigh these costs. The more value the consumer is offered, the more likely they are to buy. Low-ticket items simply do not offer the best value.

Building Trust Through Guarantees

According to eStats, the top three reasons why online consumers don't purchase are security, privacy, and trust. Specifically, the main reasons Net users don't buy online are:

1. Security: fear of credit card fraud potential and hackers
2. Fear or reluctance to disclose personal information and data
3. General lack of trust in vendor
4. Lack of adequate product information or confusing site structure
5. Lack of variety
6. Higher total order prices than offline
7. Not able to see/feel/test merchandise
8. Poor, slow, or nonexistent customer service options
9. Site pages take too long to download
10. Have to wait for delivery

Source: eStats, 1998

To overcome this, online retailers must not only provide a simple and easy way for consumers to find and purchase their products, they must convince the customer that theirs is a reliable and safe Web site, and that the product is of the quality they expect.

The problem of trust in security and product quality can be overcome in two ways. First, offering the customer a money-back guarantee on every product purchased, and second, reconfirming that the site is secure. It may even be wise to present numbers reconfirming the overall security of the site and the Internet. If you've had no problems with security, let the customer know.

In a similar way, fear of personal information being used can be easily overcome by creating a policy of nondisclosure. This can be as strong as never releasing information except to federal law enforcement officials. It can be defined as only using general demographic information to enable general site profiling. Whichever policy is established, the customer should know up front and clearly how their information will be used. Full disclosure is always the best policy on the Net.

The Post Purchase Opportunity

As with the offline sales cycle, the retailer is presented with an excellent opportunity to increase their sales by trying to up-sell or re-sell the customer. However, with the reluctance most online consumers have to the purchase process, it is best to try this after they have closed their sale. Attempting to sell before this may cause the customer to stop their purchase.

A better time to try to up-sell is just after the purchase is completed. Think about it. The customer has just purchased. They have overcome several barriers of trust to provide a credit card number and click the button. What better time to provide them with an opportunity to improve the product they just bought, or purchase an add-on that will improve its service. When the customer clicks the OK button, they are sent to another page. There is no reason this page should not say, "Thank you for your purchase, may I suggest also trying X? It would go very well with your recent buy."

SUBSCRIPTIONS

The third way to generate revenue in today's online environment is by charging consumers for entering the site. At this point in time, the only sites that are truly successful at this are adult sites and the *Wall Street Journal*. This is not to say there are not others, but the cost of entry is high.

The content itself must have intrinsic value and not be readily available anywhere else. The *Wall Street Journal* provides insight into the financial markets that consumers obviously value greatly. At the same time adult sites provide content that its customers value, albeit for very different reasons.

The problem arises when sites try to provide news or information that is readily available on Yahoo!.com or latimes.com. At this point in time, there is simply too much information and content to make many subscription-based Web sites profitable. What you may want to do is start with a subscription-based area of the site as a test. If people are willing to pay, then extend it. If not, join the ad-based model.

CONCLUSION

Making money on the Internet is less about technology and more about maintaining the shopping experience. More than any other element in an online business, generating online revenue is about applying the classic rules of business. Give the customer what they want, provide them with a painless experience, treat them special, and give them a reason to return often. If you cannot do this, no amount of technology will help you sell. Put your money in your customer, not a new cash register.

This also applies to selling advertising. Media buyers and marketing directors have thousands of sites to choose from when buying advertising. If you make their lives easier by making mid-campaign recommendations on how to improve their performance, overdelivering on ads served, providing timely reports, and having a set billing practice, they will find it easier to return.

None of this is new. The advertising wheels still work. Only the cart has changed.

CHAPTER SIX

Research and Customer Service to Enhance Communications

THE HOW AND WHY OF RESEARCH

The Internet is about information. Not just giving it away, but collecting it. Remember the two-way conversation? The only way to create one is to know who you are talking to and what they want. To know what they want and be able to deliver it turns a one-time visit into a long-term brand relationship.

No, this does not mean bombarding the person with a list of demographic questions. It does mean asking relevant questions that help you learn who the consumer is. When you know who the customer is and they know who you are, you have the beginnings of a relationship. It also means you have taken the first step toward gaining a customer for life.

The first question you will probably be asked about your site is how many people are visiting. The second is who are they. From that point on, one of the most important factors to ongoing success is not only the quantity of traffic, but also the quality. Again, to know this, you need research.

Research does not mean bombarding the consumer with a list of twenty questions regarding their gender and income. It means collecting information over time and combining that into a database which allows you to create a profile of your user.

Contrary to some misconceptions, online consumers are willing to provide information about themselves. No, they will not spend 20 minutes answering highly personal questions about their financial worth, but they will tell you who they are, and what they like. There are two important factors involved in what people will divulge. First, consumers are more willing to answer questions if they receive something in return. Second, there is no rule that says every question has to be asked only once or at the same time or through the same vehicle. This is where databases become important.

The Power of Databases

The Internet itself is about information. Not just giving information away, but collecting it. Stickiness, community, two-way relationships— all require some level of research in order to find out what the consumer is doing and what they want. Without this, you will probably only use half of the Internet's capabilities.

Think of the visual Web site as the icing on the cake. The design and content are used to attract consumers in. Beneath this there should be a database that captures customer information. This is critical to effective online marketing. This database is what enables businesses to capture everything from demographic information to qualitative information about specific products or product benefits to how well the Web site is designed or any other question that may be relevant.

The foundation of any research program is a database. The mechanisms of this database can be as simple as an Excel spreadsheet with columns of information that can be sorted to a fully functional database that provides ongoing analyses. As with most elements of a site, budgets will primarily dictate the type of database at the start. The important factor is its ability to expand and grow with your needs. As your site grows and you begin to collect more information, you will want your database to grow with you, not only in size but also in functionality. As long as the database remains consistent, you will be able to combine the responses from five different questionnaires that took place over a year. These can be compared to assess not only how your Web site has grown, but how your audience has grown.

The type of database you use will depend on what and how much information you are trying to capture. To start off with a smaller, simpler database is fine, as long as you will be able to take the information and transfer it to a larger database further down the road. Usually, this is not a problem. However, enough people forget to make this a priority when the database format is being developed and encounter a problem when trying to transfer the information at a later time.

As the old woodworking saying goes, measure twice, cut once, think ahead.

What to Ask and How to Ask It

What

Regardless of your site, there are two types of information you will need at first. The first type can be captured from your log files (informational files about your site traffic and usage). This will tell you such things as how many people are visiting, how long they stayed on the site, how much information they downloaded, where they come from, what type of platform they use and what pages they visit. There are a number of programs that allow you to capture this information. One of the most popular is called Webtrends. In effect, this allows a Web site to download its log files and analyze them. Whether this is a daily, weekly, or monthly report is a factor of how many times you want to download your log files.

The second type of information you will need is basic demographic information about your user. This is information almost any advertiser or investor will request. Providing such things as who is visiting, what they like and dislike, and what are their buying patterns is essential to driving business. The most important questions most advertisers will ask for are usually age, gender, household income, geographic location, and education level. After this, the information really depends on the site's core business.

A site selling advertising or an ecommerce Web site will probably want to know purchasing habits such as, "How much do you spend annually on shoes?" or "How much have you spent purchasing items on the Internet?" or "When was the last time you purchased a television set?" An online news service will probably want to know reading habits such as "How often do you read the newspaper?" or "What type of news is most important to you?"

In addition to demographic information and buying patterns, finding out what consumers like or dislike will become important to developing future content. Learning what hobbies the person enjoys or what publications the person reads begins to create a complete profile that not only helps you describe who your customer is, but helps you sell to them in the future. Ideally, from all the information you capture, you want to be able to build a complete customer profile and update it over time so you know exactly who your customer is.[37]

In addition to who uses a site, how they use the site is just as important. To find out how a person uses navigation buttons, locates

---

[37] See appendix 5 for a sample customer profile.

information, or responds to icons and graphics can greatly increase traffic. Consumers want to have the most pleasant experience they can. They are willing to give information if they know it will help their experience in the future.

How

As important to the questions you ask is how the questions are posed and how often they are asked. This means any consumer question should be posed as unobtrusively as possible and should be incorporated into the content as much as possible.

The first rule is never ask all of your questions at the same time. It is almost useless to ask any customer to respond to thirty questions, hoping to have an easy-to-read datasheet. First, the consumer who has the time to spend on a lengthy questionnaire is probably not your primary customer. Second, the accuracy of such a questionnaire is usually suspect, as most consumers completing such a form will invariably slip over a number of responses.

The key to creating a large database out of a series of questionnaires or surveys is to use a central locator, such as an email address that all of the responses can eventually be tabulated around. Once a database is set up in this way, surveys, email responses, and questionnaires can be combined quickly and easily.

The second rule is not breaking the consumer's experience. Like intrusive advertising, an intrusive survey breaks the consumer's experience. Having a series of questions pop up when a person clicks on a general navigation button is intrusive. Creating a specific button that sends consumers to a questionnaire is unobtrusive and puts the control in the consumer's hands. Asking a person to answer five relevant questions when entering a sweepstakes is unobtrusive. Asking a person to answer twenty questions is intrusive. For the best results, any questions should be incorporated into, and relevant to the content surrounding them. At times, content could be created to lead the consumer toward the questions of a survey. In some cases, a sweepstakes is little more than content designed to induce a consumer to respond to more questions than they normally would.

In the same vein, the consumer should be made aware of why the questions are being asked, and be reassured the questions will only be used en masse, not as a tool to market to individuals. An example of this would be prior to a site redesign. Most online consumers are more than happy to comment on a Web site and suggest ways to improve it. A Web site that states, "We are undergoing a redesign and would like your comments to help us create a better site," is more likely to get constructive responses than a site that simply asks what someone likes or dislikes about its design.

For basic information about demographics and buying patterns a survey is an excellent research tool. It creates incentives for the user to complete the questionnaire and drives a larger number of entrants than a simple questionnaire. A questionnaire is different because it does not offer any incentive to the user. These are best used as an ongoing tool that remains up on a site in order to capture ongoing user information. Yet another tool is combining questions into a registration process. However, the benefits from registration must outweigh the depth of the questions posed. For questions regarding site design and navigation, creating a contest or incorporating an online focus group may be more appropriate. Each of these methods will be covered later in this chapter.

A Pop-Up Solution

At this point, it should be obvious that online consumers do not want anything forced upon them. They want control over their travels online. This poses a particular problem with online research. Researchers want to get an accurate representation of their consumers; however, consumers are not always willing to participate. This creates a nonrandom sampling universe that makes most surveys inherently inaccurate.

As has been mentioned, there is software called Pop-up software. This software selects visitors at a pre-determined rate (e.g., every fiftieth visitor). When the fiftieth visitor clicks on a given page, a Javascript creates a window asking if that person wants to complete a short survey. If the visitor clicks yes, they are sent to the survey. If the visitor clicks no, the window disappears.

The great benefit of this type of software is that surveys can be created for the general site or for particular sections, creating a very targeted tool to test whatever part of the site is most appropriate. In addition, when used with cookies, this type of software can target women with one survey and men with another, or teens with one survey and college students with another.

At the same time, it can be incorporated into feedback programs for finding participants for online focus groups, or for applying cookies randomly. Best of all, because they are random they can provide an element of statistical accuracy to any online research.

An Ever-Changing Customer

As a site matures and as the Internet matures, the audience that visits a particular site will change. It is important to maintain current content and track these changes. They will dictate the ongoing look and feel for a Web site and its advertisers. To do this, an initial survey or series of surveys should be created to benchmark who the initial consumer is. After this a new survey should be introduced quarterly or semi-annually, depending on the growth of the site. These new surveys should repeat the basic demographic questions and introduce several new questions pertaining to consumer habits or likes and dislikes each time. The demographic questions will maintain a record of who the ongoing consumer is. The remaining questions will help to build a customer profile.

Although I doubt your customer will change greatly from survey to survey, you may be surprised to find a sudden shift in demographics either due to a change in the content, or as a result of advertising. It is these shifts that are important to making a decision of how and when the content and design of a site should change.

Building Research into the Content Development Process

Content Development

Consumers enjoy taking part in the development of a Web site. It gives them a sense of ownership over the content and creates a stronger relationship. Without asking consumers what they want, almost any Web site risks doing just the opposite and giving them exactly what they don't want. The only way to avoid this common mistake is to ask.

If a Web site is considering two different graphic designs when revising an older section, it is a simple matter to post both designs on a page and ask the person who is eventually going to be using it what they want to see. If a Web site is looking to expand the content it carries, it is an easy task to list all the options and have the consumer decide. Far too many sites simply put up content based on what they think the consumer wants rather than actually asking the consumer.

Creating an ongoing program that brings the consumer into the content development process not only turns out a product the consumer is more likely to want, it gives them ownership of the site itself.

Content Maintenance

The best time to find out what your consumer wants is when the customer is in the content itself. Yes, looking at the most visited directories section of a log file will give you some idea as to the general likes and dislikes of your customer. However, asking them while they read the content itself is far timelier and a more accurate judge of content.

Such a mechanism can be as easy as a rating system for your content at the end of every story. This can be a series of five small buttons allowing the reader to rate the content from 1 to 5, or it can include a text box where the reader can enter what they liked or disliked about the content. The important element is ease of use. The more complicated it is for the person to enter, the less they will be willing to tell.

The second most important element is telling the customer why they are being asked for information. If people are asked to "rate our story," many will simply move on. If instead it is posed as "in order to make a better site, we want to know what you thought about this story," people are far more likely to respond. Not only does this increase response, it lets the customer know they are an integral part of the site and their opinion matters.

Such elements can be placed throughout a site and implemented in various ways. Asking customers what they would like to see on the site, what they like or dislike about a design element, and how well a story met their needs, all helps you build a site that better responds to their needs. In the end, it's their site anyway. They are the ones choosing to enter or move on. Why not at least let them know you acknowledge this and even more importantly, find out what they want?

One word of caution in using any of these measures: Most of the people to respond will either be adamantly for or against what they see. Those people in the middle, the majority, will most likely not participate. Because of this, take any response you receive with a grain of salt.

RESEARCH TOOLS

There are as many research tools as there are ways to use them. It is not important to try to use all of them. Start with a simple survey to find basic demographic information. Perhaps incorporate other questions in a registration process for an email newsletter. When time permits, add an ongoing questionnaire onto the Web site's home page. After the first quarter, create a survey with additional questions. By creating a slow campaign using the different elements, your consumers will not know how much information you have gathered and compiled. Just don't try to do it all at once.

Of the tools mentioned here, the process required of surveys, questionnaires, sweepstakes, contests, and even registration are the same.

Each uses a Web page to list a series of questions for which responses are sent to a central database. Because of this and other reasons, they are best for basic quantitative information. Such elements as feedback and email questionnaires allow the consumer more time and space to complete the questions posed. For this reason, they are better used for qualitative information—to determine opinions (such as selecting between two graphic designs). Because of their unique nature, cookies and other tracking programs are best used to determine how a consumer uses a site and navigates around its pages.

Surveys and Questionnaires

Questionnaires and surveys are simply a Web page with a series of questions on it. Participants are usually invited in with a button or other mechanism and asked to complete the questions. They are best used as an ongoing tool to measure changes in basic demographic information.

They can be used for larger studies. However, each respondent needs to consciously enter the Web page with the survey or questionnaire. Only those who care enough, or dislike the site enough will enter, leaving the majority of the site's consumers unrepresented. Because of this, these tools should be used as an ongoing measure of who is visiting, not as a way to gather opinions.

One way around this is to create a random survey. In this example a pop-up window or button would appear for the Nth visitor and invite them to take the survey. Although the majority of those entering the survey will most likely feel stronger one way or the other than the average visitor, this method will better represent the majority of a site's customers.

Contests and Sweepstakes

Similar to surveys and questionnaires, contests and sweepstakes should be primarily used as a means to get basic customer information. The benefit of a contest is the prize being offered. This is a tool to attract more entrants and will represent a greater percentage of the site's population. Yes, the nature of the prize itself will sway the type of entrant; however, by carefully selecting the mix of prizes being offered, a more generic mix of entrant can be attracted.

A contest or a sweepstakes is probably not the best way to gather opinions. They will most likely be swayed by the perceived effect their response may have on the respondent's opportunity to win. In addition, the value of the prize should be taken into consideration when determining the number of questions posed. The greater the value of the prize, the more questions an entrant will answer.

Registration

The registration process and the willingness of a consumer to enter a site or a section of a site is based on one thing—the value of the content. The more benefits a consumer expects to receive, the more likely they will be to register. As has been said before, the value of creating a club or a special membership area is enormous, not only to find out information about the user, but to attract a very targeted audience. However, registration should not be created to gather information. Information should be gathered as a result of registration.

Feedback

Customer feedback is probably the best source of information about your site. It provides an ongoing analysis of your site that can be compared over time. The key is providing your customers with a way to provide constructive feedback. A "feedback" button will probably go unused until someone has a complaint. At that point, there is little more you can do but try to correct the problem. Providing your customers with a way to speak to you is essential to developing any customer driven relationship and creating a flow of feedback.

Instead of a "feedback" button, create questions that elicit a response. Asking specific questions about various aspects of the site is a good way to start. These can be placed on specific pages or included in online newsletters. Wherever they are placed, they are more likely to encourage constructive responses.

One of the most important elements to maintaining a constant flow of feedback is the ability to respond. This does not mean creating a lengthy letter answering every email. It does mean creating some type of acknowledgment the email was received and it was read. An automated response makes people feel like a computer received their comments and their efforts were for naught. If at all possible, have a human respond. Create a simple thank-you letter that says someone is reading his or her notes. Encourage them to write again and often. Post occasional emails on a section of the site.

Creating and encouraging feedback not only helps you learn about your customer, it is part of an ongoing customer service program. It not only helps the site, it helps cement a relationship with the customer. It keeps a channel open for future conversations and allows you to contact them directly. Let people know their voice matters and they will continue talking, and that is what you want.

Email

Email is an excellent way to conduct a quantitative survey. As with other surveys, an email survey is simply formatted to fit into an email. It's best not to attach a page containing the survey for two reasons. Not everyone has the same application (e.g., Word, WordPerfect) nor the same version, causing problems in formatting. More important, with the potential for viruses, many consumers are wary of opening unknown documents. However, when formatted into the text of an email, this is a quick and easy way to conduct ongoing surveys.

One of the biggest advantages of an email survey is the ability of the consumer to answer the questions on their own time. This means the entrant can open the survey, and take their time with their responses—a huge advantage over almost any other survey format. Other advantages include the ability to reach a large survey group quickly and inexpensively. However, like all email programs, permission to send the email is essential to remaining off the SPAM lists.

To conduct an email survey simply requires gathering the names of willing participants and sending them a consistent survey within the text of the email. To return the survey, respondents simply need to return the email to the sender. One note, do not try to get overly creative. Like browsers, email programs can be finicky and not everyone has the latest version. Pages sent in one format usually look different when read in another. Depending on who you are trying to reach, you may want to use the lowest common browser to reach a larger audience.

Cookies

A cookie is a text file that is used to identify a particular consumer. It rests on the consumer's browser and provides identifying information to the Web servers. Only those servers that look for the particular cookie track it. If several sites work together, it is possible for each to track the information gathered by the cookies. Cookies are generally used to identify repeat visitors and to track how a visitor interacts with the site itself.

Cookies can be used for a number of reasons. They can contain passwords to make it easier for entry into a site. They can store preferences to create personalized start pages. They can work with a shopping cart program to track purchases from page to page and over a longer period of time. They can allow you to identify who the customer is, letting you know what type of advertising would most likely interest them. In short, cookies allow a Web server to identify who the individual is that is visiting. Once they are able to identify this, they can track what their preferences are and what their habits are.

Cookies start with a line of HTML in a document, usually as a CGI script. This script sets a cookie under a given name as a text file. Each cookie has an expiration date, so that they will not continue gathering data forever.

The downside to cookies is twofold. First, some perceive cookies as a tool to spy on them. To be clear, cookies cannot gather information from a hard drive or any other element of a computer. They are a tag, an identifying tool that a browser can track, not a program that gathers information. At one point, there were security issues surrounding cookies, but at the time of this writing almost all of those security problems were resolved.

The second issue is the consumer perception that cookies are forced up on them. Contrary to popular thought, cookies are a voluntary tool. If a customer does not want a cookie, they can disallow them or erase them with the click of a mouse.

To avoid both of these issues, it is best to state exactly why you are using cookies and how they will affect your customers. Information is the best educator.

For research, cookies are best used to track a person though a given Web site, but as you will see later, when combined with a survey, a Web site can determine where younger people go, what sections males visit, or the demographic makeup of a specific area.

Focus Groups

Traditional focus groups are generally held with a number of people (usually eight to twelve). These people are brought into a room and asked to discuss a series of questions by a moderator. They will usually be watched by a group of hidden observers. The questions may change in response to answers, creating a flexible way to determine what customers think and feel about a given product.

Online focus groups are held in much the same way. Generally, six to twelve people are invited to join a chat at a specific time. Respondents then spend a predetermined amount of time discussing a specific topic. This can range from opinions about a product, a Web site, an advertising campaign, or any other subject matter.

Online focus groups have a number of benefits. The leading one is cost. Because there is no physical space needed, the only costs are in holding the chat and paying the moderator. Even better, the moderator has the ability to speak with respondents together or separately. This means the moderator can delve more deeply into a particular response without interrupting the flow of general conversation. Also, because participation in an online focus group is by invitation, participants can be selected based on a given set of criteria. Finally, because online focus groups are maintained through text, transcripts can be made available almost immediately rather than having to wait for days.

Customer Service to Enhance Communications

As competition increases and product differences decrease, customer service becomes the deciding factor in a purchase decision. Just like the sales process, customer service starts well before a product is actually purchased. As its name implies, customer service is about servicing the customer and responding to their needs. It includes everything from the way a person is greeted when they call with a question about a product to the availability of answers to frequently asked questions. Customer service is about not making the customer take the extra step.

This is no different for the publisher who is not selling a product. With such news services as the Associated Press and Reuters, much of the news we read today is a commodity—it is news service information rewritten according to the views of the publication. One year ago there were ten services delivering jokes via email. Today there are hundreds. As more publishers enter the field, customer service will be more of a defining element in keeping readers. This includes how they are treated and talked to, how their problems and concerns are answered, and how good they feel about their experience.

Customer service helps maintain an ongoing conversation with the customer after a purchase is made. It helps develop a brand that people want to stay in touch with when they consider making a second purchase.

An excellent example of how to create an effective customer service program can be found in the FultonStreet.com case study. It illustrates how simple it is to create a good customer service program and how essential that program is in creating long-term customers.

Integrating Service into the Content

Customer service should be invisible and automatic. It should not scream, "We are providing you with extra service," but should echo within the content itself. This means a banner saying thank you for paying will not suffice. A toll-free number for questions or problems is a start. A way for people to track the location of their purchase is another. A human voice to speak to when problems arise is yet another. Regardless of what is used, it needs to be incorporated into the content to create a seamless conversation. If the customer has to work to find the "customer service" area, the spell will be lost before it can even work.

Most companies think the only time they need customer service is when a problem arises but by that time it's too late. The best time to create an effective program is to introduce the customer into the service process before they have a problem. The goal is to get the customer to feel like there is someone on the other side of the computer who responds to their needs. If a problem arises with an order or with the site in general it is much easier for them to forgive a human than a machine.

How to do this? Simply open a dialogue and respond. Place a "comment" button on lead pages to provide an easy way to voice opinions. Provide a toll-free telephone number for customers to call with questions. If a customer sends an email with a question or a compliment for the site, respond to it with a human answer. People know when a response was computer generated, and their enthusiasm is usually on par with the computer that wrote it.

Just as important, recognize when a customer has made a valuable comment or suggestion. Noting when a site element was added because of a customer suggestion or comment is as important as creating the opportunity to make that suggestion. It reaffirms that the site listens and truly cares about its customers.

Yes, this will take work, but if a site shows it recognizes the value of its customers, they will be a customer for life.

Outbound/Inbound Customer Service

Customer service is communication. It provides the person with a way into the conversation that was started when they first looked at the product being sold. Effective customer service, like effective marketing should listen to what the customer wants and respond. The better the response, the better the customer service and the happier the customer.

To be effective, customer service should accomplish several things. First, it should tell the customer that they are valued. Second, it should provide the customer with multiple ways to communicate. Telephone, fax, email, postal mail, and any other ways for them to communicate should be offered. Third, it should make them feel good about their purchase.

This does not always mean sitting back and waiting for them to contact you. No, this does not mean sending a stream of emails about the product. It means asking the customer if it is acceptable to contact them with product updates, special offers, or timely opportunities. It means creating a club in which customers can voice concerns or talk about the product amongst themselves. It means telephoning the customer on a rare occasion to ask how they liked their purchase.

Tools to use in this process include email and newsletters, and on-site information that goes beyond an FAQ. To create a bulletin board exclusively for customers to talk openly is not only a powerful tool to maintain a conversation with them, it provides a forum to learn how the customer feels about your product or service and to learn what needs to change.

CONCLUSION

Creating and maintaining a customer service program is essential to the creation of an effective Web presence. It allows any Web site to continue the customer conversation that was started in the beginning of the purchase cycle.

A key element of any customer service program is an ongoing research campaign. The goal is not only to learn about the customer, but to learn what they want and be able to respond to it. Only then is an ongoing conversation possible, and only with an ongoing conversation can a one-time buyer become a loyal brand customer. And that is the goal of everything we have tried to accomplish in building an online presence.

CHAPTER SEVEN

Case Studies

CASE 1: BIKINI.COM—DEVELOPING A BRAND IN A HEAVILY COMPETITIVE MARKET

Bikini.com is unique among Web sites, not because of its content, but because it was launched as completely original content. When it started, it had no products to sell and no parent publication to support it. It truly is one of the few original Internet concepts able to develop itself into a successful brand.

Bikini.com was started by the brother and sister team of Gail and Howard Sonnenschein. Both started as television producers in the fashion and swimwear fields. Both recognized the popularity of swimsuits among men and women as not only a way to attract viewers to television programs and special magazine editions but as a lifestyle indicator.

When the site was launched in 1997, *Sports Illustrated's* swimsuit issue owned the print market and *Baywatch* owned television. Both were very strong brands in the beach category and seemingly undefeatable. Gail and Howard understood that to create a brand that would survive they would not only need to find an undeveloped niche, but find a medium that would take advantage of that niche.

With this in mind the Sonnenscheins created Bikini.com, a lifestyle-oriented consumer entertainment brand designed to go further than either *Baywatch* or *Sports Illustrated* was able to—think Disney meets the beach.

"We set out to create a product that would be the ultimate beach party featuring real people, and that would be very tastefully done and wholesome enough for parents of teenagers and for sponsors. It had to be sexy but not sexist, and it had to be fun." As Gail puts it, "Bikini.com is much more than a Web site about bikinis. It's about a lifestyle. It's not just about the beach or about bikinis. It's about fun. It takes the party atmosphere of Frankie and Annette and the old *Beach Blanket Bingo* movies and updates it for today."

Their goal was to create an online brand that could be leveraged into offline mediums including television, music, licensing, and even product merchandising. For them, the site is only the tip of the sand pile.

From its inception, it took about 2 years to develop the concept into viable content that included such potential projects as a TV series. The Web site actually launched on July 4, 1997.

According to Howard, "There was never any wavering from the original concept of creating a category killer brand—a Web site designed not as an online publication, but as the center of a brand. It was designed to build a strong brand image that would translate easily to any other medium."

Today, Bikini.com is the world's most fun and comprehensive beach lifestyle Internet site. It has a tongue-in-cheek, retro look that's lighthearted, bright and full of all-American sex appeal. It continues the tradition of other wholesome beach lifestyle media properties such as *Baywatch* without competing against it. As Howard still says, "You watch *Baywatch*, you read the *Sports Illustrated* swimsuit issue, and you log on to Bikini.com!"

Already they are closing licensing deals for everything from mousepads and posters to calendars, t-shirts, and refrigerator magnets.

Website Ad Sales and Ecommerce Hub

Creating and Maintaining a Branded Image

Maintaining a consistent look and feel is probably the most difficult part of developing any Web site. With an almost endless supply of images, colors, icons, technology, and content to choose from, the ability to maintain one creative direction throughout any Web site is a constant battle. However, as Bikini.com found, it is probably one of the most important elements in defining a brand and creating a recognizable and memorable presence.

For Bikini.com this has been the ongoing job of Howard Sonnenschein. Originally, Howard and Gail conceptualized the site with a "bubblegum-retro look," a term Howard uses to encompass a modern look and feel of 60s pop culture. "At the start, we looked at everything as inspiration—*The Partridge Family*, *The Brady Bunch*, Frankie and Annette, a plastic hula dancer, anything we could get our hands on was fair game. Not so much in actual artwork, but to generate ideas, to create a vision for what we wanted."

Before they had a staff of designers and artists working with them, Howard began by using these images to create an updated color scheme that worked for the 90s audience. "There were so many dark Web sites on the net, a lot of blacks and reds. I wanted to create something light and fun—a vacation for the mind. In the beginning I started grabbing everything I could get my hands on. If it fit into our ideal, I'd figure out a way to work it in. I knew I'd never get to what we wanted by myself, but we had to start somewhere."

Howard and Gail knew their vision for Bikini.com would be several years in the making. Without the resources other sites had available to them, they created a goal of how they wanted the site to look in 2 years. "I knew at the start we couldn't build what I wanted, so I kept the concept in my head, and began working to get there. As we added people and technology, I made sure everything fit into that goal." That way, as new technology became available they could decide what was relevant and what to avoid.

As Howard looks back, he remembers their hiring experiences. "In hiring someone, we quickly found there was a lot of good talent out there. The problem wasn't trying to find talent. It was trying to find people who shared our vision and our site's personality."

To this day Howard remembers the biggest stumbling block he had was not technical. It was people trying to change the vision he and his sister shared. However, by maintaining the concept of what they were trying to achieve, they were able to create an identifiable look and feel for their brand.

According to Howard, "The most important thing to remember is to put your blinders on and charge forward. Listen to what people say, but don't let them sidetrack the vision you have. That's the most important part of creating a brand—maintaining the vision you started with."

Today, when you walk though the offices of Bikini.com, you will see a secondary product from these efforts. A collection of movie posters, classic magazine covers, and postcards now covers the walls, and on top of Howard's computer still sits a plastic hula dancer. Everyone who steps into Bikini.com instantly knows where they are.

Leveraging the Brand

The Sonnenscheins developed Bikini.com to be a category killer in the entertainment category. To achieve this they needed to create a brand that could be expanded into just about any medium from television to print to news media. They knew the Bikini.com logo would not be enough. They needed something to embody the 60s beach culture. Welcome the Bikini.com Supermodels—a wholesome, "G" rated version of the Spice Girls.

Each has her own personality that is expanded in comic book fashion on the site, but more importantly, these Supermodels are able to take the brand offline and into other mediums.

In addition to this, Bikini.com has futher leveraged its brand by creating a line of licensed products, generating income and driving awareness through calendars, posters, videos, and other pop culture merchandise. Even more important, they have created strategic alliances with noncompeting and complementary companies such as WWF and a leading British search engine.

Today, Bikini.com remains the first online beach Web site. Portraying a wholesome attitude and growing every day, Bikini.com is the ultimate beach brand on the Net, without the sand in your shoes.

CASE 2: BLUEFLY—GROWTH THROUGH STRATEGIC PARTNERSHIPS

Bluefly.com is the child of Pivot Rules, a leading-edge golf clothing company that helped revolutionize the golfing industry by designing clothes for the new generation of golfers.

As the Internet matured, the owners of Pivot Rules began to realize the growing opportunities. They saw a ready-made audience that fit the demographic profile of the young golfer, and a tool with which to sell.

The key, they thought, was to find a way to integrate the growing Internet into its existing business model.

After exploring opportunities for online golf commerce, the owners of Pivot Rules quickly realized an even larger market existed with tremendous potential yet to be claimed. After completing some preliminary research, they found a niche within which to focus. They realized many people liked shopping at off-price and outlet stores; however, many had poor experiences. First, outlet stores were usually located outside of major cities and were often difficult to get to. Second, once shoppers traveled the distances, not only did they have trouble finding items they wanted, but finding the right colors and sizes only led to frustration. At the same time, the owners of Pivot Rules saw many online stores were little more than a purchase mechanism attached to a catalog.

Bluefly knew in order to overcome these issues, they had to go beyond just offering ease of use and low prices. They had to create a lifestyle shopping environment where people could discover new products, find tips on fashion, and feel like they were treated special. Their concept was to create a lifestyle brand that would do more than just sell brand name, end-of-season apparel, and accessories through an online retail store.

Ken Seif began developing the site in May of 1997. Knowing they brought the retail experience they needed, the principals of Bluefly.com began to search for a partner with extensive Internet experience that could integrate their unique spirit and personality. The result was a site that paid extra attention to the shopper's experience.

In order to drive traffic, Bluefly passed by the traditional online advertising campaign of banner ads and trades. Instead of trying to drive traffic to their content, they worked to create relationships that, in effect, brought their content to the mass audiences of key portal sites.

One of the first such partnerships was created with America Online in 1998, the world's leading Internet online service. In this deal, Bluefly.com would become a tenant in the apparel department of AOL's Shopping Channel with permanent links to its Web site from AOL.com.

As Jonathan Morris, executive vice president of Pivot Rules noted, "This is not only a vehicle to drive traffic to Bluefly.com but also a great branding opportunity to leverage our early entry into the online apparel category."

In addition to having tenant positions on AOL, AOL.com, and CompuServe, under the terms of the deal, Bluefly also received promotional and joint marketing benefits as well as the use of AOL key words to provide direct access to its Web site.

A second partnership was created with the @Home Network—the leader in high-speed Internet services via cable infrastructure. Under the terms of this deal, Bluefly created a co-branded version of the Bluefly Mycatalog for @Home users. This catalog allows shoppers to enter their clothing sizes, favorite brands, and favorite products, after which My-Catalog displays high quality photos and descriptions of all the items that are in stock and that match the shopper's preferences.

In November of the same year, Bluefly.com and Lycos, Inc., the second most visited Internet hub, announced a strategic alliance. Here, Bluefly was established as a premier commerce vendor of Lycos and was made accessible throughout the Lycos Network on Lycos.com, Tripod, and MailCity sites through a combination of advertising, commerce, and promotional programs.

"This was a very significant agreement for us," said Ken, chief executive officer of Bluefly, Inc. "With over 40 percent reach, the Lycos Network provided access to a diverse and fast-growing audience."

This online commerce and advertising deal included links to Bluefly from Lycos.com, Tripod, and MailCity as well as banner advertising, links from over 100 keywords and many other promotional and joint marketing components.

Other deals were similarly struck with Infoseek's GO Network, a major Internet portal designed to connect people with the things they care about most; and with Excite, Inc., a global Internet media company.

As a result of their approach, on January 28, 1999, Bluefly, just months after they opened their site, Bluefly.com, announced that its fourth quarter gross sales before returns and allowances exceeded $300,000 and were well ahead of the company's expectations.

"I was extremely pleased by Bluefly.com's first full quarter of operations," said Ken. "During this period, we saw our online store's traffic grow by 2,200 percent to 664,230 unique users for the month of December from 28,297 in September. We also saw our sales numbers increase significantly, including our average order size, but more importantly, perhaps, we started to learn about our customers and their purchasing preferences which should accelerate our ability to expand our product offering intelligently and grow our business," Seiff added.

The total number of registered users also grew by 1,556 percent to 26,048 at the end of December 1998, from 1,573 at the end of September. During the fourth quarter, the average user spent nearly 11 minutes on the site and viewed approximately eighteen pages per visit.

"Considering that our strategic marketing deals with Yahoo! and Lycos did not launch until late in the fourth quarter and that our focus during this period was to lay the foundation for a business which we hope will grow for many years to come, this has been an exceptional start," Ken said.

CASE 3:   FULTONSTREET.COM—SERVICE, SERVICE, SERVICE BEATS LOCATION, LOCATION, LOCATION

For most the thought of trying to sell fish over the Internet is an insane idea. Not for Stratis Morfogen. He comes from a long line of entrepreneurs who, for almost 100 years, have been synonymous with the fish trade in New York City.

He is the third generation to run the family fish business. His grandfather owned the famous Pappas Seafood Restaurant from 1904 to 1970 and was involved in all the buying at the Fulton Fish Market. His father opened a chain of fourteen seafood restaurants in the New York City area in the 1950s. His uncle, George Morfogen, was the buyer for the Grand Central Oyster Bar in New York City for over 20 years and introduced restauranteurs like the late Gilbert LeCoze from Le Bernardin Restaurant to the Fulton Fish Market.

"When Gilbert first arrived from Paris, no one would give him credit, and they were selling him terrible products. My uncle George took Gilbert around to all the suppliers and introduced him as his friend so that everyone would give him credit. You see," Stratis explains, "the reputation my father and uncle have are extremely important to my relationships with the top suppliers in the market. I can't afford to lose that no matter where I sell fish."

"I got the idea for FultonStreet.com from my brother. I have a lot of friends and family in land-locked areas. I had been sending filets or oysters to them for years. The business didn't occur to me until my brother, an award-winning chef in Aspen, Colorado, told him he couldn't find fish or seafood at all. 'I said Aspen, one of the richest areas in the USA, you can't find fish there?' Light bulb! That was it! I knew what I had to do! Two-thirds of the United States is landlocked, and I didn't need much more than that to go on."

At the time, Stratis didn't know that there was a ball under the mouse. Spending 12 to 14 hours creating relationships with his customers, he had never used a computer, and had no interest in them until the idea for an Internet business crossed his path. He began speaking with a number of online companies until he found a consultant who could help him. He still credits his knowledge about the Internet to Alex Demeo, the CEO of Vangard Interactive—his mentor in ecommerce.

However, the most important element to his online success is not the technology. It remains personal service. Stratis started working in the restaurant trade when he was five, first by placing lemons on plates as they went by, then as dishwasher, prep, busboy, apprentice to the chef, waiter, bartender, and manager. "When I finally got to the floor, the most important thing I had to do was to learn each customer's name, what they drank, or what their favorite foods and desserts were. When Mr. Jones came to my front door, it was 'good evening, Mr. Jones,' 'get Mr. Jones his favorite cocktail.' Making him feel good was my job. When Mr. Jones walked in with friends, I would mention his name five times before he sat down, and made Mr. Jones feel special. It's no different on the Internet. My goal with FultonStreet.com is to address each customer individually when they place an order, not like a file number."

To Stratis, this means breaking down the computer screen and making the customer feel like they are being assisted by a person, not a program. He does this by assigning each customer a personal service representative. "I want each customer addressed, and thanked personally. When they return, it's 'welcome back, Ms. Branden, we appreciate your business.'"

When a customer places an order, his service representative has the ability to send a complimentary soup or appetizer. To Stratis, the cost of that is nothing compared to what other companies spend on advertising, and his growth is proof that word-of-mouth works.

"We give our staff full authority to tell Ms. Branden, 'When your friends order, I will personally take care of them and treat them to some complimentary samples.' Those samples are the best investments we will ever make."

Fulton Street has a conversion ratio of 4.2 percent, from homepage hits to orders. In addition, their traffic currently averages 1.5 to 2 million page-views per month, with an average duration of 6 minutes and two seconds. An incredible 50 percent of his customers come back and make a second purchase within 60 days.

Stratis credits factors like top quality products, reasonable pricing, and consistent packaging and delivery to the success of FultonStreet.com. However, as Stratis insists, "Without the personal touch, it's nothing." Another sign of FultonStreet's commitment to clientele can be seen in their responses to email. While other companies respond to email in one or two days, if at all, FultonStreet.com responds instantly. If the customer is on AOL, they will even send an instant message.

"I have been asked, 'What are you doing to do next Christmas when you do 20,000 orders, instead of 3,000?' My answer is hire another twenty-five full-time customer service reps. The secret is not to get greedy and sacrifice good customer service for another 2 percent in profits."

This formula of customer service has ensured continued expansion of their service. FultonStreet.com is currently finalizing a licensing agreement with a company in Ireland to fulfill orders from Europe and the Middle East. This company will supply seafood from Ireland to ensure freshness and quality, while FultonStreet.com maintains contact with each customer. To help with any language barriers they will use a translation program and, thanks to the new currency standard, processing European orders will be even easier.

To Stratis the fact that more companies are not doing more customer service on the Internet is unfathomable. "I think the merchants jumped over the basics, or didn't work as a restaurant host at the age of 17. Success is about communication and making people happy. The customer's name is so simple to remember and it makes a customer so happy to hear it from a person, not a computer. Trust me, the consumer can tell the difference."

Like so many owners of offline companies that were moving online, Stratis started with a technical consultant. After working through the issues of building a Web site with Alex Demeo, he knew the technical issues were not the point. "Compared to opening and running a restaurant, going online was easy. But my reason for success is I didn't forget where I came from and I applied that to the Internet. Online with service, service, service—it's better than location, location, location."

Where is Stratis going to take Fultonstreet.com in the future? It all goes back to his past. "I can remember learning the fish business when I was about 5 years old. At that time, the Fulton Fish Market was a huge outdoor fish and seafood auction. My uncle George was haggling over the price of halibut one day. They had been going back and forth for at least 2 hours and were stuck with a nickel's difference in price. 'Why don't you just give him the nickel?' I asked. My uncle turns around and says to me, 'It's not a nickel; it's 485 nickels,' and, that was my first lesson in the bidding game, I never forgot it."

Now, many years later, FultonStreet.com has created a new fish auction online and has come full circle from the roots of Stratis Morfogen. It is so successful uBid has placed FultonStreet.com on its front page along with such companies as Dell Computers with a guarantee of 300 orders in the second weekend alone. How did Stratis Morfogen accomplish this in just 2 years? Treating the customer like a person.

"I received an email because of my deal with uBid several weeks ago. They said to me that none of their merchants ever send an email thanking the customer for their order nor an email to follow up on the tracking and time of delivery." Stratis recounts. "They couldn't believe we were doing that; they were shocked! And that's a major reason they are giving us exposure on their homepage. I made them change their software to include an email at checkout. They never did that before. Where else but on the Internet could you find a billion-dollar company listening to me? It is a dream."

CASE 4: TERANREALTY.COM—EXPANDING A BUSINESS BY BUILDING NEW WALLS

Before the Internet was a household word, Andrew Peck began to realize the potential that existed. Andrew had recently purchased a long established real estate firm in Woodstock, New York, whose owner was retiring. It was 1996 and the market was slow. However, even more problematic was the state of the company. It had been neglected by the previous owner and was in desperate need of revitalization.

Having worked in real estate for years, Andrew knew there was an untapped real estate market just two hours' drive south in New York City. Woodstock was, and remains an easy drive for New Yorkers looking to escape the city for a weekend, and a destination for people wanting to leave the city altogether. Trying to reach this market through traditional advertising was expensive, and most customers had more questions than one small ad could answer.

"Although we occasionally ran ads in New York City papers, for the most part people who were interested in purchasing in the area would drive up here and walk in. They might look at the local paper and call or drive by our for sale signs and stop in, but they still had to take the first step." Andrew realized the first meeting was usually spent answering questions about the area, what homes sold for recently, or how current mortgage rates would affect monthly payments. He would then spend what time there was left rushing to show several houses. So, with no previous computer experience, Andrew began looking at his online opportunities.

"There were cheap fixed-format real estate Web sites which had no appeal to me. They were catalogs which never quite provided the kind of information I knew first-time buyers wanted. I interviewed a number of people who designed Web sites and found someone who I thought could execute my ideas within my budget."

It didn't take much time to realize the potential. Andrew's Web site provided more than just pictures of available properties. Because house hunting in Woodstock usually necessitated an overnight stay, Andrew provided information about local bed and breakfasts and restaurants. He also included calculators that estimated monthly mortgage costs and information about property taxes and local schools. In essence, *www.teranrealty.com* became an information resource for potential customers.

Of importance to Andrew was the look and feel of the site. He wanted it to be more practical than flashy, more a reflection of the office itself than a showcase of leading edge technology. Today, TeranRealty.com reflects the look and feel of the office itself. "The site is a direct response to the reason most people are interested in buying property in Woodstock itself—to get away from the high-tech pressures of the city." The design is simple and low-key, and most important very easy to navigate.

Of equal importance, TeranRealty.com was created to respond to questions most new home buyers were asking. By providing information about interest rates, local taxes, mortgage calcuations, and monthly ownership costs, Andrew was able to create a relationship with potential buyers before they even rented a car—weeks before other local real estate businesses even had a chance to speak with them. "By the time the customer gets to our door, they already have a good feeling about us. They are loyal to us because they know we can do more than just sell property, we can help. And that is an extremely important thing in our business." Andrew admits there is no way to replace personal contact with a new customer, but his Web site saves him time in serving new clients because it is able to answer the most common questions.

Has it been successful? "It is successful beyond my expectations." In the 2½ years of operation, the cost of building, maintaining, and updating it has been roughly $10,000. "Without question the site has paid back the investment several times over. It has become the source of more than a third of our buyer customers, many of whom have praised it."

Just as importantly, the Web site has been an excellent way to attract home sellers as well. Being recognized by the International Real Estate Digest as being "excellent," the Web site is an important reason in having a seller choose their firm to represent them.

After looking at the Web site a customer will usually email, telephone, or fax their interest about a particular property. Andrew's staff will usually speak with the customer to better find out what they are looking for and to create a more personal dialogue. They will fax down pictures and descriptions of other homes the customer may be interested in. This way, the customer can spend more time looking at potential properties and less time thumbing through books. Even after a customer leaves, Teran Realty can stay in touch through email and faxes to notify them about the properties they looked at or even about new properties on the market.

"There will never be a substitute for spending time in person with clients in our business. Email and fax simply make our job more efficient."

By providing more than just an online catalog of homes, Andrew has found a very effective way to extend the reach of his company and build a relationship with his customers before they even pull off the highway. Best of all, he has been able to do this without sacrificing the personal service his company is built on.

He has done all of this by building a Web site that augments his relationship with his clients rather than tries to replace it.

CASE 5:   PAINTINGSDIRECT.COM—BUILDING RELATIONSHIPS TO SELL ART

PaintingsDirect.com was founded after an entrepreneur's frustrating attempt at purchasing art from traditional galleries. Two years ago, Christine Bourron, its founder and CEO, set out to purchase a painting for her mother's birthday. Her criteria were simple enough. She wanted it to be an original work of art by an American artist and she wanted it to contain a bouquet of flowers.

After spending several weekends visiting art galleries in a number of cities, she was unable to find the painting of her choice. The experience made her realize several things. First, the art world was not a place for the uninitiated; second, there were few opportunities to buy original works from galleries for under $5,000; and third, there were probably many others out there who, like her, wanted more on their walls than mere framed posters but simply did not know how or where to find them.

Christine started to research how people bought art and soon realized the potential size of the opportunity. Lots of people were interested in art but either did not know where to purchase it, or didn't consider themselves "sophisticated" enough to make the "right" decision or simply could not afford it. Instead, they were content to purchase cheap posters and spend hundreds of dollars on framing them. The key to being successful in this market was being able to provide people with a genuine selection of original art at reasonable and attainable prices without the intimidation of a gallery. The opportunity to create a Web site to accomplish this became immediately clear.

Realizing that the creation of an easy-to-use source for art was the most important first step in establishing this online business, she initially ignored all the possible bells and whistles and instead focused on four primary objectives:

- *Developing an easy to use Web site*—the site had to be simple, elegant, and easy to understand. True to online conventions, buttons were clearly marked on the left side of the page and the home page was easily accessible from any point on the site.
- *Minimizing download time*—since PaintingsDirect.com was going to be an image intensive site, downloading was kept to a minimum in order to guarantee an enjoyable experience.
- *Maintaining element of style*—the site had to reflect the quality of art within it and maintain the look and feel that consumers associated with art.
- *Ensuring easy searching*—recognizing that online visitors would be frustrated if they could not easily find what they were looking for, Christine designed a search engine that the customer could use to find a painting based on almost any criteria, ranging from artist, to style, to color scheme, to price range, and even country of origin.

When the site was launched, Christine initiated a dialogue with her potential customers. She began by asking visitors what they wanted to see on the site. She found many wanted to know more about the artists whose works they were viewing. She realized this was an advantage she possessed over galleries. By providing a rich source of information about the artist including their personal motivations behind each work, PaintingsDirect.com could forge a link between the customer and the art.

She started to provide customers with a wealth of relevant information about each artist and every painting. Not only did this succeed in establishing a connection between the artist and the customer, it also helped customers feel as though they were making a more informed purchase. As a result, they become more comfortable with their purchase.

Speaking with customers also taught Christine that providing information about the artists alongside the work itself helped to decrease returns. Today, even after a purchase is completed, PaintingsDirect.com includes a biography of the artist with the shipped painting. One customer returned a painting she did not want anymore but ended up purchasing a painting that was more expensive.

The comfort this customer experienced was fostered by providing information about the art and the artists, keeping her up-to-date on new artists, and being flexible with returns.

"It was the painting that didn't work, not the service. We've found that styles change, but good service and information always remains important."

Christine admits the biggest difficulty she encountered was trying to convince artists to show their work online. "Initially it was very difficult to convince American artists to work with us. In retrospect, PaintingsDirect.com was introducing a brand-new concept into a very traditional market. The artists were very wary of their reputations and of having their works shown online. Once we began working with European artists who were anxious to access the United States market, American artists became aware of how we promoted our artists and were more than willing to come on board. But until we established our own reputation, it was a struggle."

Today, PaintingsDirect.com continues to build relationships with artists and customers by providing information and protecting the interests of its artists and its customers. With an inventory of art that most museums would be jealous of, Christine Bourron continues to build her business by ensuring customers can find what they want, quickly, easily, and without restrictions to price, style, or taste—truly an idea whose time has come.

Web Sites to List

The following are leading Web sites to list your home page and section pages. Although this is not a complete list, starting your efforts here will cover most primary consumer searches for information.

Directories

The following directories are primary information retrieval sites. Not only should home page URLs be listed, but individual URLs from primary site segments should be listed. Some directories will include links very quickly, others, such as Yahoo!, may take time to evaluate the site. Plan on it taking an average of 4 weeks to be listed in directories.

555-1212.com	BizWiz
ClickIt!	Global On-Line Directory InfoSpace
LinkStar Internet Directory	Net Mall
Starting Point	Yahoo!

Search Engines

Search engines are very similar to directories, except they use programs such as "spiders" to search for and evaluate Web sites. Even though this is performed automatically, it is important to submit home page and segment URLs to these search engines to ensure they visit your site.

Alta Vista   Docking Bay

Excite   Infoseek Guide

HotBot   Lycos

WebCrawler

What's New Sites

These are well-known sites that highlight the newest Web sites on the Internet. Although they change constantly, a listing on any of these sites can effect an increase in traffic.

Advertising Site of the Day   Cool Site of the Day

Coolynx of the Day   Funky Site of the Day

Internet Magazine's What's New   Macmillan Web Site of the Week

NCSA's What's New   Net Happenings

Project Cool Sightings

Minor Directories

Although minor directories have fewer listings, they usually provide a more targeted search. This makes them an important element when listing your Web site.

BizCardz   BizWeb

Delta Cool   Delta Design's Business Directory

Encyclopedia of Links   Four11.com

GTE Superpages: I-Explorer
   WWW submission   IndoBiz

Internet Explorer

Online Information Resources

The following are Web sites that will provide you with an updated series of resources for information:

News about the Internet

- Current news about the Web—*www.newslinx.com*
- News of Internet trends—*www.nua.ie/surveys*
- The standard—*www.thestandard.net*

Email Lists and Newsletter Information

- Direct email source list—*www.copywriter.com/lists*
- Internet advertising discussion list—*www.Internetadvertising.org*
- Postmaster direct—*www.postmasterdirect.com*
- Listz—*www.listz.com*
- PAML—*www.neosoft.com/Internet/paml*
- Ezines—*www.dominis.com/Zines*

Online Advertising Magazines and Information

- AdAge—*www.adage.com*
- AdWeek—*www.adweek.com*
- Brandweek—*www.brandweek.com*
- ClickZ—*www.clickz.com*

- Iconoclast—*www.iconoclast.com*
- The Rant—*www.olaf.net/rant/rant.html*
- Online advertising discussion list—*www.o-a.com*
- Microscope—*www.pscentral.com*

Online Marketing Discussion Groups and Lists

- A sponsor-supported discussion list that creates a network of expert and beginning online marketers and consultants— *www.exposure-usa.com/i-advertising/.*
- List sponsored by LinkExchange to discuss online advertising and marketing issues—*www.linkexchange.com.*
- wwwac.org contains a number of lists on a variety of online issues from advertising and law to imaging and graphics—*www.wwwac.org.*
- The latest Web site promotion developments, opportunities, and tips affecting your Web site, by the guys who literally wrote the book on guerrilla marketing—*www.gmarketing.com.*
- An email newsletter about online advertising—*majordomo@iconocast. com.*
- This site has daily updates and news on the Internet industry— *www.merc.com.*
- An online source of major Web launches and events. Matched by topic. This is only sent to Internet media editors, writers, reporters, and site reviewers—*www.urlwire.com.*

Groups and Organizations

- American Association of Advertising Agencies— *www.commercepark.com/AAAA*
- American Advertising Federation—*www.aaf.org*
- Association of Interactive Media—*www.interactivehq.org*
- American Marketing Association—*www.ama.org*
- CASIE (Coalition for Advertising-Supported Information & Entertainment)—*www.commercepark.com/AAAA/casie/index.html*
- CommerceNet—*www.commerce.net*
- Internet Advertising Bureau—*www.iab.net*
- New York New Media Association—*www.nynma.org*

- Web Designers and Developers Association—*www.wdda.org*
- Webgirls—*www.webgrrls.com*

Tips for Online Advertising

- ClickZ—*www.clickz.com*
- Eyescream Interactive—*www.eyescream.com*
- GreyInteractive Canada—*www.hawkmedia.com*
- Hays Interactive Marketing—*www.hays.com*
- i-Frontier—*www.i-frontier.com*
- K2 Design—*www.k2design.com*
- Tenagra Corporation—*www.tenagra.com*
- Thunderhouse Online Communcation—*www.thunderhouse.com*

Online Marketing and Sales Information

- Strategies, techniques, and resources for business-to-business Web marketers—*www.netb2b.com*
- Banner ad size standards—*www.iab.net/iab_banner_standards/ bannersource.html*
- Internet marketing and statistic site—*www.cyberatlas.com*
- All the information you need for working with and around search engines—*www.searchenginewatch.com/*
- Internet registration services with InterNIC— *www.networksolutions.com*
- A networking resource for online advertising, marketing, and site development—*www.channelseven.com*
- The 1996 hotWired advertising effectiveness—*www.hotwired.com/ brandstudy/*
- *http://www.clickz.com/index.shtml*—An excellent resource for doing business online
- Demographic and computing data—*www.statmarket.com*
- Complete resource for online advertising/marketing/sales information—*www.advertising.utexas.edu*
- An excellent resource for Web marketers, with a wide range of information about online advertising—*www.olaf.com*

Statistics and Demographics

- Demographic and computing data collected from more than 25,000 Web sites—*www.statmarket.com*
- Statistics and information updated daily and weekly for Internet marketers—*www.emarketer.com*
- An online marketing firm that keeps a large array of online statistics and information—*http://www.websidestory.com*
- One of the best ongoing surveys of Internet users I have found—*http://www.cc.gatech.edu/gvu/user_surveys*
- Updated lists of data, studies, and statistics about online business and advertising—*www.cyberatlas.com*

Technical Resources

- Jumbo.com (300,000+ shareware files)—*www.jumbo.com*
- Builder.com (programming codes)—*www.builder.com/*
- List of ISPs by country, state, area code, or zip—*www.thelist.Inter net.com*
- All about cookies—*www.cookiecentral.com*

Creative and Design Resources

- Web design tips and secrets—*www.ei-web.com/*
- Resource guide for designers and developers—*www.designshops.com/*
- An excellent source for clip art—*www.cliptoart.com*
- Yet another source for art resources—*world-arts-resources.com/artists/artist-a7.html*
- Standard banner ad sizes—*www.iab.net/iab-banner-standards/bannersource.html*
- Salary and development costs—*http://www.planetx.org/~jenn/producers/salary.html*

Advertising Resources

- A searchable database where you can find the best places to advertise your products around the world—*www.adbase.net*

- A list of online associate or affiliate programs to add revenue to your Web site—*www.associateprograms.com*
- Information about ad networks, brokers, reps, pay-per-click ads, pay-per-sale / partner / commission programs, ad serving software, banner exchanges, counters and trackers, log analysis—*www.adbility.com/WPAG*

Content Resources

- Providing syndicated content for travel, news, gold, horoscopes, and more to add to sites—*www.timeslink.com*
- Offers free customized and automated news feed for Web sites and a list of syndicated content sources—*www.isyndicate.com*
- Dedicated to helping new developers design their Web sites, complete with tips and links—*www.colinmackenzie.org/webdesign/*
- A great resource for finding tips and hints on developing online Web content. It even contains links to content exhanges—*www.contentious.com*
- Interesting study for Web writing/reading—*www.useit.com/alertbox/9710a.html*

Third Party Services

Auditing

- ABC: provides audits and verification services to ad-supported sites—*www.accessabc.com*.
- Ipro: Collects, analyzes, and measures site activity—*www.ipro.com*.
- BPA: Third party audit organization that verifies traffic—*www.bpai.com/audits*.

Personalization

- Art Technology Group: Provides Internet solutions for creating personalized content—*www.atg.com*.
- Firefly: Provides software for creating personalized communities—*www.firefly.net*.

Traffic Measurement and Analysis

- Accipiter: Solutions to track individual visitors and their activity—*www.accipiter.com*.
- AdCount: Provides summaries of a Web site's activities—*www.netcount.com*.
- WebTrends: Software packages to self-measure site traffic—*www.webtrends.com*.
- SurveySite: Online research software including pop-up—*www.surveysite.com*.

Ad Server Programs

- Ad Smart: Software to serve and track onsite advertising—*www.adsmart.com.*
- DoubleClick: Software to serve and track onsite advertising—*www.doubleclick.com.*
- NetGravity: Software to serve and track onsite advertising—*www.netgravity.com.*

Ad Servers

- Accipiter: Standard ad management technology with profiling capabilities—*www.accipiter.com.*
- AdKnowledge: Complete system automating ad serving/reporting process—*www.adknowledge.com.*
- NetGravity: Provides the ability to manage, deliver, target, etc.—*www.netgravity.com.*

Summary Overview of Web Ad Rates[38]

Summary Info Updated 6/9/98

Search Engines—
Range—$20–50 CPM
Benchmark—$20–40 CPM

Keyword Advertising—
Range—$40–70 CPM

Local Advertising—
Range $20–$80 CPM

City Guides—
Range—$20–80 CPM
Benchmark—$50 CPM

Advertising Networks $10–$70 CPM

Auction Sites $1–$25 CPM

Top 100 Web Sites—
Range—$25–$100 CPM
Benchmark—$30–$75 CPM

---

[38] Special thanks to AdKnowledge, http://*www.marketmatch.com* for access to their MarketMatch ad rate guide.

Opt-In Email Advertising $.10–$.20 per address

Small Targeted Content Sites—

Range—$10–$80 CPM

Benchmark—$30–$70 CPM

Sponsored Content $45–$85 CPM

Beyond the Banner—

New Models that Break the Mold—$35–$100 CPM

Click-Through Pricing—$.20–$1.20

Range of Click-Throughs—.5%–15%

Average Click-Throughs—.5%–2.5%

Research Studies—Average ctr .89%–.96%

Overall Average CPM—$27

Average CPM by Category—Lowest $22.66 for shareware sites to $62.44 for audio sites ($250 for "episodic" sites)

Pay Per Lead—$1–$15

Pay Per Sale—5%–30% of purchase price

Online Audience Lifestyle and Consumer Behavior Summary

- **Age:** 45–54
- **Gender:** Male
- **Lifestyle**

International traveler	Frequent Flyer programs	
Ski/tennis	Golf	
Raquetball	Sail	Scuba dive/snorkel
Country club	Health club/gym	Attend theater
Donate to PBS	Go to bars/clubs, movies, football and hockey games	

- **Products and Services**

  Drycleaning   Buy computer books

  Own cappucino maker   Use olive oil

  Buy gourmet coffee beans   Buy hardcover books

  Buy designer jeans   Own convertibles, station wagons

  American Express card   Buy dance, New-Wave, classical music

  Have $100k+ life insurance   Own a piano

  Stocks, home equity loans, money market funds, annuities

  Drink hard alcohol, imported beer and wine, low alcohol beer, imported wine, bottled water, cordials, liqueurs

  Own pagers, PCs, VCRs, answering machines, CD players, cameras, stereo equipment

  Own Lexus, Honda, Acura, BMW, Toyota, Mercedes

  Eat Grape Nuts, Kellog's Special K, Wheaties

- **TV Viewing Habits:**

The Tonight Show	David Letterman	
ABC World News	Face the Nation, MacNeil/Lehrer News Hour	
60 Minutes	The Movie Channel	The Disney Channel
HBO	Lifetime	Learning Channel
Siskel and Ebert	College football	C-Span
Arts and Entertainment		

- **Radio Listening:**

  Talk and news radio

  Classical, soft rock, jazz, progressive rock, adult contemporary radio

- **Popular Publications Read:**

Travel and Leisure, Inc.	*Fortune*	*Money*	*Forbes*
Food and Wine	*Bon Appetit*	*Gourmet*	*Elle*
Business Week	*Newsweek*	*Time*	*Smithsonian*
Vogue	*Self*	*GQ*	*Golf Magazine*
PC World	*Rolling Stone*	*Omni*	
Boating	*Runner's World*	*Tennis*	
Town and Country	*Metropolitan Home*		

  Newspaper sections: Business, science/tech, life, and style

Sample Barter Agreement

What follows is a sample contract for a barter or content share. It is purposely designed as an open-ended agreement rather than a contract. If you are creating a content share, replace the banner levels with the content you will be trading. This is intended to provide you with an outline for your business dealing. All use of this agreement should be pursuant to conversations with a legal representative.

Name

Company

Street Address

City, State

Dear XXX,

To facilitate a barter agreement, we propose the following terms:

[Company name] will provide [Partnering company name] with 1,000,000 advertising banner impressions (Complete page views with your ad banner and link to your site) within [Site URL]. This will commence on [Date] and end on [Date] (Advertising period).

In return, [Partnering company name] will provide [Company name] with 1,000,000 advertising banner impressions (Complete page views with a [Company name] ad banner with a link to [Company URL]) on [Partnering site URL].com commencing on [Date] and ending on [Date] ("Advertising period").

Impressions will be provided by both parties on a space available basis. Any shortfall in performance by either party will be "made good" to the other party within the 60 days following the close of the Advertising period.

Both parties will provide the other with their current advertising performance reports, weekly, or as requested, until completion of the Advertising period. If either party must provide a "make good," additional advertising performance reports will be provided to the other party weekly, or as requested, until the agreed upon number of impressions has been delivered.

No money will change hands and no invoices will be created by either party. This is simply a barter of advertising by the parties.

Either party may terminate this agreement at any time upon 48 hours notice. Upon termination, each party must calculate the total impressions delivered, and the party that has delivered the fewest impressions must make up the difference to the other party within 60 days through providing advertising space for the number of impressions equal to the difference. Reporting will be produced on a weekly basis, with reports showing impressions, click throughs, and click rates for each ad.

Ads are subject to approval by both parties and will be no larger than 468 pixels wide $\times$ 60 pixels high (Not to exceed 10K byte size).

The terms of this agreement shall be kept confidential to both parties. The advertising outlined above is nontransferable. Both parties have the right to audit the books of the other party to verify number of impressions. The auditor must be reasonably acceptable to the party being audited. Audits must take place during ordinary business hours and only after 10 days written notice.

If this proposal is acceptable, please countersign this letter and return it to me at [Fax number].

The proposal will be revoked if you have not returned a countersigned copy to me before [Date].

Sweepstakes Official Rules[39]

1. SPONSOR/PRODUCER

[Web site]'s Sweepstakes ("sweepstakes") is sponsored and produced by [Company name].

2. ELIGIBILITY

No purchase necessary.

The [Web site] Sweepstakes is open to all people who reside in locations where the entry of such a contest is legal and lawful. Odds of winning are determined by the total number of entries received. If entrant is under 18, entrant must have parent's permission to play. Employees, officers, directors, shareholders, agents, representatives, and the immediate family members of companies providing prizes and producer, and their parent companies, affiliates, subsidiaries, and advertising, promotion and legal advisors, are not eligible to participate. Void where prohibited by law.

In the event this sweepstakes is compromised in any way, electronically or otherwise, that is beyond the control of the producer, the producer reserves the right to withdraw the transmission of this sweepstakes and award the remaining prizes among entries received prior to the date of the withdrawal.

---

[39] This is intended as an example of a sweepstakes' rules. It is not intended as a legal document. Please consult your lawyer before running a sweepstakes as the required rules differ according to county, state and country.

3. HOW TO ENTER

No purchase or subscription to an Internet service provider is necessary. For purposes of this promotion, an "entrant" shall consist of a person, family, or household with a valid email address for Internet or email entry or valid household mailing address for an entry by regular mail. Duplicates, copies, and other mechanical reproductions are not permitted. Illegible, mutilated, or incomplete entries will be disqualified. Each entry must be mailed separately. Mail-in entries must be received by midnight of date posted on [Web site URL].

Producers are not responsible for lost/stolen/postage due mail or late/misdirected mail, phone calls, or Internet entries; failed, incomplete, or delayed transmission of Internet entries or for problems with computer, on-line, telephone, or Internet communications or damage to user's system as a result of participating in the sweepstakes. Illegible/incomplete entries will be disqualified. All entries become the property of the producer and will not be returned. False or deceptive entries or acts will render entrants ineligible.

There are two ways to enter the sweepstakes.

Entry by Computer Players may enter the sweepstakes by using a browser to complete the [Web site] registration form, located at [Web site URL]. All computer entries must be received by the deadlines set forth in paragraph 4. Entries generated by a script, macro, or other automated means are not eligible.

Entry by Mail Online entry not necessary. Participants can enter via regular mail by hand printing your name, postal address, email address, telephone number, date of birth, gender, occupation, and household income on a 3" × 5" card and mailing it to: [Web site] [Address].

4. TIMING OF SWEEPSTAKES

The sweepstakes begins at 12:01 AM Eastern Standard Time (EST) on [Date], and ends 11:59 PM Eastern Standard Time (EST) on [Date]. Posted start and end dates for particular prizes will be posted on [Web site URL].

5. PRIZES

Five (5) prizes will be awarded to five (5) randomly selected winners. Each winner will receive one (1) [Prize].

All prizes will be awarded. Some of the prizes being awarded in this promotion were purchased by [Web site] for use as prizes. The manufacturers of these prizes are not associated or affiliated with, nor have they endorsed, [Web site] or this promotion. Any trademarks used in this promotion are the property of the respective trademark owners and are used herein for identification purposes only.

Limit one prize per household or organization per channel per week. Limit one prize per winner per month.

6. SELECTION OF WINNERS

On or about the posted end date, winners of the prize will be selected in a random drawing from all eligible entries received. Random drawings will be held under the supervision of [Company name], whose decisions are final in all matters relating to this sweepstakes. Odds of winning a prize will be equal regardless of method of entry. All prizes are guaranteed to be awarded.

No substitutions by winners for prizes. In the event a substitution for a prize becomes necessary due to unavailability, a prize of equal or greater value will be substituted at the sole discretion of the producers. Prizes are not transferable or redeemable for cash. All federal, state, and/or other tax liabilities are the sole responsibility of the winners. Acceptance of a prize constitutes permission (except where prohibited) to use winner's name, likeness, and statements for publicity purposes without additional compensation or limitation.

Odds of winning will be determined by the number of eligible entries received from Internet and regular mail entries combined.

7. NOTIFICATION OF WINNERS

All prize winners will be selected in a random drawing from among eligible entries, held on or about the posted Sweepstakes' end date. Winners will be notified by email and/or regular mail. The prize winner does not need to be online at time of notification. Winners will be required to complete and return an eligibility certification, which must be signed by the winner (or parent/guardian) and received by [Web site] within 14 days of date of notification attempt or an alternate winner will be selected in a random drawing from the pool of eligible entries. Winners, if under 18, must have a parent/legal guardian execute the Release of Liability form on their behalf. If the producer does not receive a reply to the notification announcement from the winner within 14 days, the prize may be forfeited and an alternate winner may be selected by a subsequent random drawing.

The prizes will be awarded within approximately 3 weeks after all required proof and documentation is received. If any prize notification or any prize is returned as undeliverable, the prize will be awarded to an alternate winner from the pool of entries.

All taxes on prizes, including income taxes, and any incidental expenses associated with collection of a prize are the responsibility of the winner. Winners assume all liability for any damages caused or claimed to be caused by participation or by any prize and release producer from any such liability. Acceptance of prize constitutes permission (except where prohibited by law) to use winners' name, city, state, likeness, and/or voice for purposes of advertising, promotion, and publicity without additional compensation.

8. CONDITIONS

The sweepstakes is governed by these official rules. By participating, entrants agree to these official rules, and understand that the results of the sweepstakes are final in all respects. All decisions regarding the sweepstakes including, but not limited to scoring and winner selection will be made by the producer, whose decisions shall be final.

All federal, state, and local laws and regulations apply. Void where prohibited/restricted by law. Employees and their families of [Company name], its respective affiliates, subsidiaries, parent companies, agencies, and participating retailers are not eligible.

The producer may prohibit you from participating in this sweepstakes or any future producer game if, at the sole discretion of the producer, you repeatedly show a disregard for producer rules, or act (i) in an unsportsmanlike manner, (ii) with an intent to annoy, abuse, threaten, or harass any other player or producer representative, or (iii) in any other disruptive manner.

The winners are solely responsible for all applicable federal, state, and local taxes. All federal, state, and local laws apply.

By participating in the sweepstakes, entrants agree to release and hold the producer, [Company name], [Web site].com and prize companies, as well as their respective employees, parent companies, affiliates, subsidiaries, participating retailers, and agencies harmless from any and all losses, damages, rights, claims, and actions of any kind in connection with the sweepstakes or resulting from acceptance, possession, or use of any prize, including, without limitation, personal injuries, death, and property damage, and claims based on publicity rights, defamation, or invasion of privacy. Further producer is not in any manner responsible or liable for any warranty, representation or guarantee, express or implied, in fact or in law, relative to any prize, including but not limited to its quality, mechanical condition, or fitness for a particular purpose.

Winner assumes all liability for injuries caused or claimed to be caused by participation in this sweepstakes. Producer reserves the right in its sole discretion to cancel or suspend this sweepstakes should virus, bugs, or other causes beyond the control of the producer corrupt the administration, security, or proper play of the sweepstakes. Producer is not responsible for computer system, phone line, hardware, software, or program malfunctions, or other errors, failures, or delays in computer transmission or network connections that are human or technical in nature. Producer is not responsible for incorrect or inaccurate entry information whether caused by Internet users or by error of the equipment or programming associated with or utilized in the sweepstakes or by any technical or human error which may occur in the processing of the entries in the sweepstakes. If prize notification is returned as undeliverable or producer cannot contact winners for any reason, prize may be forfeited. Winners may be required to sign and return an affidavit of eligibility and a liability/publicity release within 14 days of notification or prize may be forfeited.

The sweepstakes may be terminated without prior notice; however, prizes will still be awarded. In the event of early termination of the sweepstakes, all prizes will be awarded in a random drawing from among all eligible entries received through the date on which the sweepstakes is terminated.

11. TO FIND OUT WHO WON

For the name of the prize winner of the [Web site] Sweepstakes, visit the main game page [Web site URL]. Winners' names will be posted for 60 days after the completion of the sweepstakes drawing. Or send a self-addressed stamped envelope to: Winners List, [Web site], [Company name], [Address].

Sponsorship Proposal Outline

Proposals should incorporate text and graphics. The goal is not to provide a potential client with an in-depth description of a site. It should act as a teaser to the site and generate interest. Ideally it should be no longer than 8 to 10 pages, text should be bulleted to highlight key points, and screen shots should be used only to provide an example of the site's better qualities and layout. Overall, it should take no longer than 10 minutes to get through. Any more time than that and it risks landing in the round file

The following example is for a college Web site trying to attract a college loan company

Page 1: Title Page (Sales line for what the sales program will do for the advertiser)

Title Text–   Bringing [Advertiser name] and the college achiever together

Body Text–   None

Graphic–   Client logo, Web site logo

Page 2: Overview Page (A general overview of what the site is about)

Text–   Delivering the A+ college student

Body Text–   Launched to provide the college achiever with the information they seek

The most complete resource for every stage of a student's life from finding a school, to financing their higher education, to searching for a career

6,000,000 page views every month

High brand association with leading online publishers

Graphic–   Home page screen shot

Page 3: Demographic Page (Bulleted demographic information)

Title Text–   Not just students, A+ students

Body Text–   Pure demographic numbers for age, gender, income, education level, geographic location, and buying/spending patterns

Graphic–   Pie charts and bar graphs to illustrate the customer

Page 4: Content Page (Brief description for each of the site's main content areas)

Title Text–   Content for every phase of a student's career

Body Text–   Getting into school—how to apply, what colleges want to know

                         Financing your education—how to pay for your education

Studying and partying–   The best way to ensure you get the most out of your college years

Job search–   What to do with your degree once you graduate

Graphics–   Thumbnail images of site's main section pages

Page 5: Sponsorship (Full outline of sponsorships offered with pricing)

Title Text–   A sponsorship designed to drive your business

Body Text–   Full year partnership with category exclusivity on a leading site

Banner placement on all pages—10 million impressions ($10 cpm)	$100,000
Fixed logo placement in lead content areas—2 million impressions	$ 20,000
Creation of branded content to promote advertiser products	$ 30,000
How to pay for college	
How to manage college debt	
Inclusion in customized emails sent to college and university faculty	added value
Logo placement in print campaign in college newspapers	added value
ANNUAL TOTAL:	$150,000

Page 6: Co-Sponsorship Page (Full description of co-sponsorship opportunity)

Title Text–   A co-sponsorship designed to drive your business

Body Text–   Full year partnership on a leading site

Banner placement on all pages—5 million impressions ($10 cpm)	$ 50,000

Fixed logo placement in select lead content areas— 500,000 impressions	$ 5,000
Creation of branded content to promote advertiser products	$ 20,000
How to pay for college	
Logo placement in print campaign on College newspapers	added value
ANNUAL TOTAL:	$ 75,000

Page 7: Co-Sponsorship Page (Full description of co-sponsorship opportunity)

Title Text– A co-sponsorship designed to drive your business

Body Text– Full year partnership on a leading site

Banner placement on all pages—5 million impressions ($10 cpm)	$ 50,000
Fixed logo placement in select lead content areas— 500,000 impressions	$ 5,000
Creation of branded content to promote advertiser products	$ 20,000
How to pay for college	
Logo placement in print campaign in college newspapers	added value
ANNUAL TOTAL:	$ 75,000

Page 8: Information Page (Contact information)

Title Text: For more information on how we can create a customized sponsorship to meet your needs, contact us directly:

Body Text: Name

Address

Phone Number

Fax Number

Email Address

Co-Branded One-Sheet

The following is a sample one-sheet for proposing a co-branded sweep-stakes. It can be used for the development of a micro-site or any other project that requires delivering basic project information. This example is for the development of a co-branded sweepstakes to promote a travel section.

It is a sales tool. As such, it should promote the realistic benefits and costs of a proposed partnership or micro-site, but it should also sell.

Overview

The following is an outline for the creation of a co-branded sweepstakes between [Host site] and [Partnering site]. The goal of this is to generate awareness for both properties and generate revenue through sponsorship opportunities. It will leverage the upcoming travel section on [Host site] as a theme for the sweepstakes.

The sweepstakes shall run for three weeks from [Start date] through [End date]. During this time, entrants will complete a basic entry form. Winners will be selected from a random drawing from the database of entrants.

Prizes will include:

- Travel from anywhere in the continental United States to [City]
- 2-day stay in a [City] hotel
- 2-day car rental in [City]

Benefits

This sweepstakes is designed to drive traffic, generate revenue, and enhance the editorial value of participating sites. In this way, a win-win-win situation will be created between the partnering sites, their customers and all participating advertisers.

[Host site] and [Participating site] will benefit by enhanced traffic, paid promotions, and revenue opportunities.

Advertisers will benefit by the creation of a targeted opportunity to reach their customers. Consumers will benefit by the chance to win prizes.

Design and Navigation

The co-branded area will be created and hosted on [Host site]. It will be linked from both the [Host site] and [Partner site] home pages. The lead page for the sweepstakes site will contain a list of prizes and an overview of the sweepstakes. In addition all questions for entry into the sweepstakes will appear on this page.

This page will link to:

- Rules Page—providing all legalities for the running of the sweepstakes
- [Host site] Overview Page—providing an overview of the [Host site]
- [Partner site] Overview Page—providing an overview of the [Partnering site]
- Prize Page—providing a complete listing of sponsors and prizes

The [Host site] will be responsible for the creation and hosting of the sweepstakes.

Timing

The co-branded sweepstakes will launch on [Start date]. It will run until [End date].

Promotions for the site in the form of [type] will begin running on [Start date] and commence until [End date].

Marketing

In order to adequately promote the sweepstakes, both Web sites shall promote the co-branded sweepstakes both online and offline. This will include:

- Both Web sites shall promote the sweepstakes on their home pages for the duration of the sweepstakes.
- Both Web sites shall run 500,000 banner ad impressions promoting the sweepstakes on a Run-Of-Site basis.
- 1 full-page print ad will run in the following newspapers [List newspapers] at an estimated cost of [Total cost].
- A co-branded press release shall be issued on behalf of [Participating sites and sponsors].

Sales

Both [Host site] and [Partnering site] will be able to sell sponsorships to the co-branded sweepstakes. Prior to selling, [Host site] and [Partnering site] will define which advertisers each may approach.

Commissions due the sales force shall be the responsibility of the closing site. In addition, a revenue share shall be implemented between the [Host site] and [Partnering site] as follows:

- Site closing sale—60%
- Partnering site—40%

Sponsorship packages shall include:

- Logo representations on sweepstakes page
- 100,000 banner impressions on [Host site]
- 100,000 banner impressions on [Partnering site]
- Sponsor description within sweepstakes page
- Entry link from sweepstakes page to sponsor site

Costs

All costs associated with the design, development, and management of the sweepstakes will be paid for by the [Host site]. All marketing and promotional costs will be split on a 50/50 basis between [Host site] and [Partnering site]. All costs involved with sales efforts will be absorbed by the various sales department of both sites.

Index